Opening with the raw, transparent honesty of one who has made the journey through grief, Doug delves into the faith that sustained him during that journey. This journey has led Doug to the place where he knows his position on grief. As a person who has worn multiple hats in my career—professional clinical counselor, licensed chemical dependency counselor, pastoral counselor, spiritual director, and now director of student affairs—I echo Doug's position that counselors, pastors, Stephen ministers, and all persons comforting those in the midst of grief must first be comfortable with grief. This book is scripturally and theologically sound. It is also a book that will wrench your heart. I invite you to take the journey with Doug, digest the Humpty Dumpty syndrome, and take his four sermons to heart. You will be forever changed!

Dr. Elaine Bednar
Director of Student Affairs
Ashland Theological Seminary

The Lord has moved in powerful ways through Doug's words. He has performed a masterful job of connecting the love of God and the healing power of his Word to the real-life pain involved in his wife Marie's death. His writing honors God, honors Marie, and opens a genuine window of hope for any person who is willing to peer through.

Eric Abel, MA
Director of *The Harbor* Ministry
Bethel Baptist Church
Savannah, Ohio

One will *not* find within the pages of *Faith, Hope and Grief* well-meaning yet unsatisfying, shallow comments that many people feel the need to dump on the grieving. Missing from these pages are the flowery platitudes comprised of dubious theology. Doug has clearly walked the long, hard, and lonely road of grief. There is no attempt to sugar coat or smooth over grief. So many people, including professing Christians, seem to be uncomfortable with grief and with those who grieve. This book demonstrates that even Christians have to deal with grief; it is a part of life and a part of the walk of faith. Even faithful Christians experience times of doubt and extreme sadness. *Faith, Hope and Grief* is full of Scripture—the Psalms in particular—that helped Doug endure extreme grief and suffering. But Scripture is not used as a bandage attempting to cover a gaping wound. Doug points out quite effectively that grief in its most raw form is found within Scripture. The Bible does not try to run from grief or downplay it. Instead it deals with the reality of it honestly.

Faith, Hope and Grief shares the journey of one man's grief in the way it really unfolds in a person's life. However, the book does not leave the reader in despair. It invites the reader to draw from the deep well of Scripture to find hope in the midst of grief. In addition, there is a helpful place to journal following each chapter so the reader can process what he or she has read. As a pastor of a congregation, I highly recommend this book and believe it will be an invaluable resource to anyone who is experiencing a time of grief in his or her life or is trying to help someone who is going through grief. In my opinion, there has not been a more helpful book in dealing with grief and suffering since C. S. Lewis's *The Problem of Pain*.

Matthew R. Potosky, MDiv
Pastor, Albion Brethren Church
Albion, Ohio

Faith, Hope and Grief

Finding God's Presence in the Midst of Crisis

DOUGLAS KNOX

WESTBOW
PRESS
A DIVISION OF THOMAS NELSON

Copyright © 2012 by Douglas Knox.

All rights reserved. No part of this book may be used or reproduced by any means, graphic, electronic, or mechanical, including photocopying, recording, taping or by any information storage retrieval system without the written permission of the publisher except in the case of brief quotations embodied in critical articles and reviews.

Scripture references are paraphrased from the King James Version.

Scripture quotations taken from the New American Standard Bible®, Copyright © 1960, 1962, 1963, 1968, 1971, 1972, 1973, 1975, 1977, 1995 by The Lockman Foundation. Used by permission." (www.Lockman.org)

Scripture taken from the Holy Bible, New International Version®. Copyright © 1973, 1978, 1984 Biblica. Used by permission of Zondervan. All rights reserved.

WestBow Press books may be ordered through booksellers or by contacting:

WestBow Press
A Division of Thomas Nelson
1663 Liberty Drive
Bloomington, IN 47403
www.westbowpress.com
1-(866) 928-1240

Because of the dynamic nature of the Internet, any web addresses or links contained in this book may have changed since publication and may no longer be valid. The views expressed in this work are solely those of the author and do not necessarily reflect the views of the publisher, and the publisher hereby disclaims any responsibility for them.

Any people depicted in stock imagery provided by Thinkstock are models, and such images are being used for illustrative purposes only.
Certain stock imagery © Thinkstock.

ISBN: 978-1-4497-6327-5 (hc)
ISBN: 978-1-4497-6326-8 (sc)
ISBN: 978-1-4497-6325-1 (e)

Library of Congress Control Number: 2012914663

Printed in the United States of America

WestBow Press rev. date: 10/04/2012

For Marie

Contents

Part 3: Hope Triumphant

Preface

Of the nine members of our Hospice support group, only Michelle and I had buried spouses. Neither one of us desired to be considered with more respect than the rest, but the other members afforded us a sense of reverence that bordered on awe. Now, five weeks into the sessions, Pauline, who had lost "only" her mother, began to succumb to the torment raging inside her. Her face contorted with emotion. She said, "I haven't been able to cry for two years. My mother was eighty-three and lived a full life. We had a wonderful relationship, and she was supposed to go. What right do I have to feel this bad in light of what *you've* had to go through? I don't want to cry."

She buried her head in her hands, and silence hung over the room.

I realized Pauline had felt unworthy to vent her feelings. Only Michelle or I could give her consent to let go of the chokehold she had on them. I waited to see if Michelle had noticed the cue, but the silence continued. I told Pauline, "You have our permission to cry."

The room remained quiet. Then Pauline's shoulders began to shake as she started to whimper. Finally she crouched into a fetal position and sobbed.

Her complaint captured the anguish we all felt—the disconnection from our loved ones, the world, and even ourselves. The confusion, guilt, and anger. The inability to make sense of our own emotions.

No wonder they call it grief.

None of us wishes this journey on anyone, but we're grateful at the same time for the ones who have taken it before us. We draw strength from their stories.

In light of that, I offer mine. I was the editor for a Christian blog site when my wife, Marie, and I learned that she had stage-four colon cancer. Marie's cancer claimed squatting rights in our lives.

Our journey with the disease entered the blog. Along with our day-by-day experiences that had been grist for the weekly devotional essays, I began to share our struggles with my readers. The blog became my vent. I found myself writing about both our high and low points and sharing feelings I couldn't speak out loud. I wrote about our pain, our frustration, and even our laughter.

It's funny how that works. Life, even when it's bad, is inseparable from itself. One day it's normal, and the next it's—well—life or death. Ultimately the cancer essays came to stand as a collection on their own. *Faith, Hope, and Grief* is the anthology of the landmarks in my journey.

The material in this book follows two strains. The dated essays are contemporary to our experiences and appear in the order in which they occurred. The four sermons appear in their logical places in the narrative, but they represent much later thinking, after I had time to process my theology. Together this collection represents my committed opinion that our theology comes from both life and thinking. A meaningful theology of suffering in particular is something that must grow from the trenches as well as the textbooks.

Finally let me speak a word on why I published this book. This is not the first book on grief, and it does not try to be the best. It's just my attempt to help anyone I can along the way. During my own grief journey, I found great comfort from those who either had gone through similar circumstances already or who were at the same stage as I was. The words, "I understand—I've been there," became salve to my heart. Now I have the opportunity to offer a measure of comfort to others.

In that light, I offer these thoughts on the faith that drove Marie and me to confront the disease, the hope that upheld us throughout our mutual ordeals and continues to uphold me, and the grief that shaped me after she died.

—Doug Knox

Part 1

Faith and Hope

Sunday, November 24
Discovery—the Journey Begins

Faith at the Foot
of the Mountain

Though he slay me, yet will I trust in him.

—Job 13:15

It was always the *C* word—something other people had to face. It was like the three-car pileup on the I-480 outer belt that the local helicopter jock reports with no more concern than a tour guide pointing out the local landmarks.

The *C* word had hit some of my friends, and I tried to empathize with them. Even then it was a vicarious sharing.

Now it has come to us, and while it may not have epic significance in a worldwide sense, it has left us breathless. A mountain has sprung up overnight where a plain lay the day before. I find myself perusing the hats and wigs in chemotherapy fashion catalogs with more than a cursory interest. I'm not sure what's going to happen, but my wife, Marie, and I will need every ounce of our faith to face it.

Last week, Marie woke up with abdominal pain so severe it doubled her over. I called work and told them I wouldn't be in, and then I took her to the emergency room. The nurses, usually more concerned about paperwork than the emergency at hand, brought out a chair and wheeled her to the back before the receptionist handed my insurance card back to me.

I completed the paperwork, collected my card, and went to the waiting room. Cushioned chairs lined two of the walls, while a low wood table piled with children's books occupied a corner. A younger lady was there already. We nodded to each other. I sat, not wanting to engage in any form of conversation. From the television mounted near the ceiling a morning talk show droned on, more distracting than entertaining. Near the television set, the wall clock read six-thirty. I perused through the assortment of magazines on a display rack.

Mostly back issues of *Cosmopolitan*, *Vogue*, *Redbook*, and *Ladies Home Journal*. A few issues of *Sports Illustrated*, and one *National Geographic*. Ignoring them, I stared at the television. At ten minutes to seven a nurse wheeled out the woman's young son and advised her on a prescription for what looked like a case of the flu with dehydration. The trio left.

By 7:20 the worry demanded more than what the television show was able to counter, and I grabbed the *National Geographic*. I couldn't concentrate on the articles, and settled for the pictures and captions. Exhausting those, I traded the magazine for a *Sports Illustrated*. This magazine's fate was little better than the *National Geographic*. The normally top-of-the-class sports articles failed to connect with me.

A couple came in and sat across from me. The husband wore a makeshift bandage on his hand, but he appeared to be in good spirits. A few moments later a nurse came out and announced a name I didn't know, the final syllable lilting up in the form of a question. The man got up and followed her to the back. After a while he came back wearing a hospital bandage, and the couple left together.

The time was eight o'clock.

I was alone in the room again. I determined to stay until word on Marie arrived, and to avoid looking at the clock. I got up and paced. A more thorough perusal of the magazine rack revealed *Good Housekeeping* and *People*. I ignored these and began to walk the lobby. The vending machine area occupied me long enough to read through the snack and drink selections. I wandered into the family meeting room, larger than the waiting room. A nurse came by and smiled. To my relief, she refrained from asking if she could help me. I wandered back to the waiting room and checked the time. Nine-forty.

The clock crept forward. Nine-forty-five. Nine-fifty. Nine-fifty-five.

At ten o-clock I decided I would wait five more minutes and then go home.

Ten-oh-five arrived and I headed for the exit door. No one watched me leave. No one ran to the window to call, "Mr. Knox?"

At home I performed activities to camouflage the fretting—cleaning, small errands, anything to keep my mind busy. By two in the afternoon, I couldn't stand the anticipation any longer and called the hospital.

"We were just going to call you," the person on the phone said. "You need to come in and talk to us."

The tone was too serious, too businesslike, to be a billing question. I rushed back to the emergency room, wondering whether they had been waiting for me to call.

A new receptionist, a lady in her late fifties, had started work and didn't recognize me from the morning visit. With the wary tone of one who expected yet another healthy patient with psychosomatic symptoms, she asked if she could help me.

I introduced myself and said my wife was in the back.

The drained expression on her face was palpable. She turned around and spoke to someone in the back, and within seconds, a nurse came to the door. She was short, with dark hair, and looked altogether too young to be a full-fledged nurse. Where the receptionist was abrupt, the nurse was almost obsequious, falling all over herself to be pleasant.

"Thank you for coming in so fast," she said with a smile that I could tell was forced. She led me to a room and pointed. "Your wife's in here."

I joined Marie, who had an IV protruding from her arm. Transfusion and saline bags hung from the stainless-steel pole behind her. A minute later, the attending physician joined us. He told us about the tests they had run and said that her hemoglobin was two pints low. Then he said, "I'm afraid we have bad news. You have cancer."

The word sliced through us like a scalpel. The doctor explained that the CAT scan showed masses in her colon and ovaries that had metastasized to her liver and ovaries.

Tears welled in Marie's eyes as she squeezed my hand. "Why didn't they catch it at the beginning of the year?"

He didn't know. The CAT scan that they had performed then didn't show anything unusual, and the blood tests were negative. They'd attributed her discharge to an active hemorrhoid.

I tried to be brave for her while we attempted to absorb the news.

The hospital transferred Marie to inpatient care and later that night sent her to the James Cancer Research Hospital on the Ohio State University campus. Now we stand at the confluence of history already written and history yet to be. After a week of tests and joint consultation, the team there believes they were dealing with colon cancer. Tomorrow they'll perform surgery, and then they'd know more. The thought hadn't escaped me that tomorrow I might know how many weeks or months Marie has to live.

These men and women hold her life in their hands. They don't strut, but they do walk with confidence. I need that right now. They've become my Team Hero—the elite combatants who will go in and extricate the silent enemy. Rationally I know we're in for a long conflict, and I can handle only one step at a time. Emotionally I'll be rooting for them while they're in surgery. Take every cell out. Do a biopsy on it if you have to, and then burn it. It's killing my wife, and I hate it.

Obviously I put a lot of stock in these men and women. But I'm also praying to the God whom Marie and I both worship. Our prayer is not a contingency plan to hedge our bets in case the surgery doesn't work. Biblical faith recognizes that our thinking must be grounded in the infinite, eternal God of creation. Solomon wrote in the Proverbs, "The fear of the Lord is the beginning of wisdom" (Proverbs 9:10). The honor we accord our God is the lens through which we understand the world around us—the means of comprehension that recognizes God's sovereignty regardless of the outcome. In other words, it calls us to say with Job, "Though he slay me, yet will I trust in him" (Job 13:15).

Both my wife and I love God's Word, and we embrace it as a matter of habit. Where I took solace in the Job passage, Marie went to the book of Daniel. The other day she told a friend over her room phone, "I guess this is going to be my lion's den." She's right. Daniel faced the lions alone in a sealed pit, with only his God to protect him. As much as I'll be with Marie in my heart, I won't be with her in the operating room. She's going to fight this one with her God at her side.

I can't boast about how strong I am right now. Frankly, the way I beg God to spare the woman I've loved for twenty-five years makes my faith look pretty shaky. The thought that I might have to let her go terrifies me. I think about an empty house and bed and wonder how I'll be able to face it.

Certain things are ours, however. We know God is sovereign. He rules by his will, which is neither evil nor capricious. His plan for our lives existed from eternity, and he will carry it out through the gravest of circumstances.

We know we can trust the surgical team because God created an orderly cosmos. Even after sin brought things like cancer into the world, his creation is still good. "I will praise you," David wrote, "because I am fearfully and wonderfully made" (Psalm 139:14). The surgeons know the intricacies of God's human creation far better than we, and we trust them with the details.

We also know that God gives us the freedom to continue to pray. I will not cease to exercise it. But this freedom is not a *carte blanche*. Even my present level of desperation forbids me to go beyond certain bounds. Because God is infinite, eternal, and unchangeable, I forfeit any right to plea-bargain. I can't demand anything from him. Marie is God's gift to me, and our times together are in his hands. Our faith requires us to live by these principles, even as we claw our way up the mountain.

We have no choice but to scale it. Granite walls reach as high as we can see, and few handholds or footholds present themselves. My fingers and toes are numb already, and we have yet to clear the first escarpment. I don't know whether we will finish the climb together or if Marie will go into eternity ahead of me. But this one thing I do know: however our God chooses to work, he remains faithful, and his love remains eternal.

Though he slay her, yet will I trust in him.

Journal

What mountain have I had to face or do I face now? How has it challenged my faith? What truths hold me up? What knowledge can I own in order to meet my mountain?

_____

_____

_____

_____

_____

_____

_____

_____

_____

_____

_____

_____

_____

Saturday, January 3

One and a Half Months after Discovery

Adventures in Cooking:
Doug Makes Lunch

"Sell me your birthright this day," Jacob said.
Esau said, "Behold, I am at the point of death. What profit will my
birthright be to me?"
And Jacob said, "Swear it this day," and he swore unto him. So Esau
sold his birthright to Jacob. Then Jacob gave Esau bread and pottage of
lentils, and he ate and drank, rose up, and went his way. Thus Esau
despised his birthright.

— Genesis 25:32-34

I am so proud of myself. For the first time in my adult life, I've broken the
five-finger cooking repertoire. Until now I could count the entrées or combos
I was capable of making on one hand: grilled cheese with tomato soup, baked
beans with franks, fried-egg sandwiches, French toast, and potato pancakes.
Now, thanks to Kraft and Taco Bell, I can enlist a second hand to catalog my
culinary savvy.

My breakthrough took place at our local Save-A-Lot store. Marie, who was
struggling after last week's chemo, asked me to get some fresh pineapple—one
of the few foods she can eat. I entered the store intent on the single item, but
as I walked through the door, a display rack filled with red boxes caught my
eye: Taco Bell Home Originals burrito dinners. I picked one up and looked at
the back. They were only two and a half bucks and had instructions that even
a kitchen semi-literate could follow. Wow, cheap *and* easy. Besides, I had the
kitchen to myself. As I read the directions, I anticipated my advancement to a
new culinary plateau. I could almost hear the invisible celestial choir bursting
forth in rapturous chorus to celebrate my discovery.

I could do this.

A surge of confidence welled up within me. I took the box with me and headed back to pick up the shredded cheese and pound of hamburger the instructions called for. My anticipation grew as I strutted down the aisle. Three ingredients from different parts of the store. Wow. I was actually cooking.

I dove into my creation as soon as I got home. While the hamburger and seasoning mix fried, I unfolded the tortilla and put it on a plate. It wasn't very impressive, but what did I expect for $2.50? I opened the can of Taco Bell refried beans and read the instructions. "Step one: Place a heaping tablespoon of refried beans on the tortilla."

Come on, a tablespoon? Refried beans define the burrito. I smeared half the can on the tortilla, figuring I could always pick up another later. Step two instructed me to add a spoonful of the hamburger seasoning mix. I drained the meat and dumped a larger-than-spoonful heap on top. Then I added another.

Step three read, "Add the shredded cheese." No problem there. I heaped cheese on the top of the hamburger until the meat was no longer visible and then threw on a couple spoonfuls of sour cream for good measure. The instructions continued, "Add the Taco Bell Zesty Red Sauce." I tore back the foil, waiting for the first whiff of pepper, and . . . nothing. The anticipated aroma never came. I lifted it to my nose and sniffed. Not even a buzz. So much for zesty. I went to the cupboard for my bottle of *Picante Habanera de Mexico* green sauce. Marie calls it the Green Death. I drizzled some on, relishing the acrid tang as the sauce blended with the other ingredients. Now that was more like it.

Then came the punch line at the end of the paragraph: "Wrap the tortilla tightly."

Wrap? Gimme a break. How was I supposed to roll all this? They hadn't given me enough tortilla. A person could put the thing on a saucer and still see the rim of the plate around it. I left the tortilla flat and decided I would have to develop my own man-size tortilla recipe.

Creative cooking—what a rush. I wonder if the Cooking Channel has any openings.

Unlike me, the ancient twins Jacob and Esau knew how to fend for themselves in the kitchen. That was about all they had in common, however. They were paternal twins, as different as two brothers could be. The minutes-older Esau, whose name meant "Red," was covered in ruddy-colored hair when he was born. He grew up to be an outdoorsy guy. As a hunter and survivalist, he learned to make a mean venison stew. His brother became known as Jacob, the Supplanter. While Jacob lacked his brother's outdoor skills, he grew to understand the intricacies of human character and became a virtuoso in manipulation and greed.

Of course the brothers fought. Even before they were born, they gave their mother Rebecca nightmares. When Rebekah asked the Lord why her pregnancy was so troublesome, he told her that she was carrying two mutually antagonistic nations in her womb (Genesis 25:22-23).

One of the two recorded turning points for both Jacob and Esau came when Esau returned from an unsuccessful survival trek, teetering on the brink of starvation. Esau begged his brother for some of the food he was cooking. Jacob, never one to miss an opportunity, finagled Esau's birthright as payment for the food. The Scripture at the beginning of this chapter tells the story. Jacob held out the carrot, and Esau bit. He was going to die. What good would a birthright be if he weren't alive to claim it? From that moment on, the Bible snubs Esau as a villain who traded an irreplaceable possession for a Happy Meal. In the Scripture's words, he despised his birthright.

This calls us to pause for a moment. Isn't that judgment a little harsh? After all, Esau was on the brink of death—at least the way he told it.

To answer that question fully, we need to think more factually than emotionally. Really, was Mr. Outdoorsman so incompetent that he actually ran himself to the brink of starvation? I don't think so. Rather, I believe this whole episode was a God-directed test of Esau's faith—a situation that drove him to two logical choices. Choice number one called for him to look beyond his immediate needs, value what belonged to him by birth, and trust God for his ultimate preservation. Choice number two drove him to cave in to his impulses. Eat now, pay now. The meal was just a birthright away.

Though his circumstances made the second choice look more reasonable, Genesis judges otherwise. When the Bible calls for faith, it sometimes calls us to exercise our trust in God when all the circumstances fight against us. This doesn't mean taking a swan dive into the blind faith abyss while we holler, "Catch me, Lord!" Biblical faith is reasonable, even when it's difficult.

So what exactly was a reasonable call to faith in this whole scenario?

Three distinct events lay within Esau's immediate purview. First, he doubtless had the testimony of his grandparents, Abraham and Sarah, who conceived Esau's father Isaac miraculously (Genesis 15, 18). This was a landmark event in the family's history. Second, Esau's mother, Rebekah, also conceived Esau and his brother only after his father Isaac had prayed for divine intervention (Genesis 19-21). In other words, two generation who existed only because of God's miraculous intervention told him that God had a plan for this family. Finally, he doubtless would have known about God's word to his mother when she was pregnant with the twins:

> Two nations are in your womb,
> And two different peoples will come from you.
>
> (Gen. 25:23a).

If God had destined Esau to become a nation, he wasn't going to die a bachelor.

With everything he had going for him, Esau should have thought in the epic terms under which he came into being. Yet he traded the significant for the immediate. He saw himself only in the present. In his mind, his birthright was nothing more than a bargaining chip. Instead of reflecting the faith he should have had, it became a symbol of the heritage he failed to understand. When he threw his birthright away, he left his mark on biblical history from that day on.

The book of Hebrews draws on the deeper application of Esau's tragic life. In this book, the author urges his wavering Jewish readers to remember their profession of faith in Christ. Regardless of the outward circumstances, they needed to remember their spiritual calling and legacy. The author said they needed to be careful, "Lest there be any fornicator, or profane person like Esau, who for one morsel of food sold his birthright. For you know that afterward, when he would have inherited the blessing, he was rejected, and found no place for repentance, though he sought it with tears" (Hebrews 12:16-17).

The issue with the blessing became the second great turning point in Jacob and Esau's lives, and came years later, when Isaac was near the end of his life. In the Genesis account, Jacob stole the blessing in an even more ruthless way than when he took Esau's birthright. But the book of Hebrews views matters differently. The reason Esau failed to find the blessing later in life was because he had made himself unworthy earlier.

Now worthiness doesn't mean he deserved it less than he had before. Worthiness is never an issue with grace. If it were, none of us could be saved. The issue was that at the time of the hunger test, Esau counted grace beneath his consideration. But when he did so, he threw away more than he realized.

We all hit times when we're consumed by hunger, whether it's for food or any other of the multitudes of passions that can ravage us in a moment. They may be perfectly legitimate in themselves. Physical passions, though, have a penchant for causing spiritual nearsightedness. One of the marks of spiritual maturity is our ability to keep our eyes on the prize and guard against sacrificing the eternal for the immediate.

Journal

In the midst of the urgent, what tempts me to try to manipulate my circumstances? What biblical realities teach me to wait for God to act?

_____

_____

_____

_____

_____

_____

_____

_____

_____

_____

_____

_____

_____

Friday, January 24

Two Months after Discovery

Out-of-Country Living

And the leper who has the plague shall tear his clothes and shave his head, and he shall put a covering upon his upper lip, and cry, "Unclean, unclean!" He shall be defiled all the days he has the plague. He is unclean. He shall dwell alone, and his habitation shall be outside the camp.

—Leviticus 13:45-46

Two months ago, our family left the normal world for Marie's post-operative care after abdominal surgery and chemotherapy.

And quarantine.

I never really understood the gravity of the word until she started going in for her chemo treatments. Granted, cancer isn't contagious, but the cure is treacherous. For forty-eight hours after her treatments, we're not allowed to touch her or any liquid bodily discharge. Nothing. I can't even kiss her. The people at James Cancer Hospital told us to buy latex gloves to use when we clean after her.

The reason for the precautions is the chemo's potency. It's a serious drug. Cancer is cell metabolism run amok, and the chemo attacks fast-growing cells. That explains why people lose their hair during their treatments. Hair grows faster than other tissue.

Since there's no way to do clinical studies, no one knows what chemo would do if a healthy person were to ingest it. Scenarios run from brain damage to liver failure. So we quarantine Marie after her Thursday treatments, and for three nights a week—the nights I most want to be there for her—she and I sleep apart from each other. Though she never complains, I rue my inability to comfort her. Sunday evenings—the nights when I can join her again—are always too far away.

I wonder, though, if my dismay is a fraction of the dread that went through Old Testament family members' minds when one of their own developed an infected boil or a festered hair follicle. In the Old Testament, leprosy was a ceremonial issue—a matter of cleanness. Whenever it occurred in the Bible, it was a symbol of God's judgment, either directly or by association.

Therefore, unlike ordinary diseases, leprosy symptoms required people to go to a priest for diagnosis. Leviticus, the book of holy living, devotes two long chapters to the process—106 verses altogether.

Leprosy laws were unflinching. If, for example, a boil broke into the tissue beneath the skin and the hair turned white, the person was leprous. The priest would pronounce the person unclean, and he would have to leave his family to dwell outside the camp. Even if the hair failed to turn white, he wasn't in the clear. The priest would have to isolate him for seven days and then reexamine him to determine the pronouncement.

Imagine a mother's dread throughout the week when her children asked, "Is Dad sick? Why can't we see him?"

Then, at the end of the quarantine, when the worst came to pass, she would have to gather her little ones into her arms and tell them, "I'm afraid I have bad news. Your father's not going to be coming home anymore." Then he would be remanded to an area outside the camp.

The words "outside the camp" held appalling religious significance. The leprosy laws came down during the wilderness wanderings under Moses, when the nation pitched their tents around the tabernacle. The symbol of God's presence was at the center of the camp, so being sent outside meant being cast away from God's presence.

God demanded a pure people, and lepers were unclean by definition. Further, anyone who touched them would become defiled. Hence, lepers were commanded to call out to anyone who approached them with the words, "Unclean, unclean!"

Leprosy was only one of the many conditions that restricted people from God's habitation. Though the law provided for God's presence among his people, it was unable to bring the people into his presence. The law showed a thousand ways to keep the people from God, but its capability to draw then near was conditional.

That was the beauty of God's Son, Jesus Christ. Those who were shut out by the law found welcome in him. Mark's Gospel tells of a leper who ignored the leprosy laws and burst through a crowd to beg Jesus to heal him. Our Lord did much more. Mark wrote, "And Jesus, moved with compassion, put forth his hand and touched him, and said, 'I will. Be clean'" (Mark 1:41).

I wonder how far apart the crowds parted when the leper, reeking of decaying flesh, hobbled through their midst and bowed before Jesus. I also wonder how great the collective gasp was when Jesus reached out and touched this man who was legally untouchable. Most of all, though, I wonder about the depth of the emotional healing that was gained from the first deliberate human contact this man had in years. This was love beyond anything the law could comprehend.

Luke 8 tells another story of a woman who battled a bloody discharge for twelve years. The disease had sapped her health, robbed her life savings, and even stolen her privilege to worship in the temple. She too pressed through a crowd, but her goal was to be surreptitious. If she could but touch Jesus' robe, she knew she would be healed.

She succeeded, only to have Jesus turn around and say, "Who touched me?" The question forced her hand, and she came forward and confessed everything. But his inquiry was not a rebuke. It was Jesus' way of affirming her faith and showing her that grace, not thievery, had saved her. He blessed her and sent her away whole.

So what does this tell us about the Old Testament? The lessons from Leviticus were not about how mean-spirited the law was, but how radical corruption is. Like Marie's cancer and chemotherapy treatments, it is the disease—not the law—that separates. Therefore, though I hate what the chemo does to her, I gladly give her up to it in exchange for the life it gives. Without it, she will die.

The law does the same thing. It shows us our sin in unflinching terms. In the end, though, that's good news, because it drives us to Christ. He who is holy himself grants forgiveness to all who come in faith. His touch takes away our decay. The author of Hebrews expressed it this way: "For by one offering he has perfected forever those who are sanctified" (Hebrews 10:14). Notice the words "has perfected forever." In the book of Hebrews, the verb "to perfect" means to bring to completion. The author of Hebrews reaches both back into history with the words "has perfected" and forward to eternity with the word "forever." He signifies completeness in every sense of the word.

Christ's work has done everything, and nothing else ever will need to be done. His work on the behalf of sinners will stand throughout eternity.

We may have destroyed ourselves through a lifetime of sinful practice. Or we may be victims of abuse, having been doomed to live with emotional shredding that occurred at someone else's hands. These don't matter to Christ. Regardless of how ugly our wounds are, his arms are open to embrace us. He said, "Come unto me, *all* who labor and are heavy laden, and I will give you rest" (Matthew 11:28). He who touched the leper and vindicated the woman with the discharge will do no less for us.

Journal

What wound torments me? What can I do to present it to Christ? How do I know that his grace is greater than my wound?

Saturday, March 8

Four Months after Discovery

Problems, Prayers, and Providence

The sons of Reuben, the Gadites, and half the tribe of Manasseh numbered forty-four thousand seven hundred sixty—valiant men who were skillful in war, able to bear shield and sword and who were able to shoot with bow, that went out to the war. They made war with the Hagarites, with Jetur, and Nephish, and Nodab. And when they began to fall before the Hagarites, they cried out to God in the battle. He heeded their prayer because they put their trust in him.

—1 Chronicles 5:18-20

Marie reached a milestone of sorts this week. She's halfway through her chemotherapy treatments—six down and six to go. As we knew they would, though, they're beginning to take their toll. Two weeks ago she thought she was over the top when the cancer indices in her blood test revealed a more than 50 percent drop from its peak levels just after her surgery. Then last week her white-cell count dropped to a level too low for the hospital to administer another treatment. She cried and said, "I just want this to be over."

That was when I realized on a gut level just where she is in this disease. Intellectually I know how serious the disease is. We both know she might not be here next year at this time. But when I witnessed the emotional defeat that broke her so soon after her victory, I was able to see the situation from her perspective.

I have the luxury of going to work and putting her sickness out of my mind for a few hours. I have outlets. Marie works, rests, and sleeps with pain. She eats, hoping the meal will stay down, and knowing if it doesn't, she is that much closer to losing the edge her metabolism needs to keep her immune system functioning. She suffers during the last few hours after one pain prescription wears off and then has to lie on the couch for another hour after she takes the next to keep it down. Her weeks begin and end on Thursdays, when she goes to Columbus for her chemotherapy treatments.

For her, the situation is always in her face. It's nothing but grave. Her battle has lasted at least since the beginning of last year, when the bleeding and pain began. Sixty-two weeks. Four hundred thirty-four days. Ten thousand four hundred hours in constant torment from a disease that is determined to kill her.

I know one thing with certainty. When I pray on her behalf, I can't begin to approach God the way she does. She is like the Reubenites, Gadites, and Manassites who cried out to God in the middle of battle. The Scripture passage at the top of this chapter occurs in the middle of the genealogical section of 1 Chronicles. For anyone trying to read through the Bible, it's one of the most-dreaded sections in the Old Testament—eight chapters of names, many unpronounceable. Keilah the Garmite, Shimon, Eshtemoa the Maachathite. Our Western eyes glaze as we read them.

They're there for a reason, though. They put teeth in the historical documents and show us that the history is real. And occasionally they add a bit of historical interlude, such as the battle in which Reuben, Gad, and Manasseh's tribes engaged with their combined army of almost forty-five thousand. The account doesn't tell when the battle happened, but it is a reasonable assumption that it occurred during Joshua's Conquest.

Numbers 32 mentions the same three tribes at the very end of the wilderness wanderings on the eve of the Conquest. With the nation yet to cross over to the west side of the Jordan River, the tribes of Reuben, Gad, and Manasseh came to Moses and requested that they be given the eastern land to settle and put down roots. They also promised to assist with the mission before them. "We will cross over armed before the Lord into the land of Canaan, but the possession of our inheritance shall remain with us on this side of the Jordan" (Numbers 32:32).

They led the charge into Canaan, fighting until Joshua congratulated them for a job well done and sent them home. Apparently, though, one of the battles turned against them. When the Chronicles mention the event, the text says, "They cried out to God in the battle" (1 Chronicles 5:20c).

This is an instructive statement. Soldiers traditionally pray before the battle because when the fighting starts, all the concentration goes there. If they had to take time to cry out to God, their tactical advantage must have gone horribly awry. But that was the moment when God chose to shift the momentum and give them victory. The text declares plainly, "He heeded their prayer because they put their trust in him" (1 Chronicles 5:20d).

Their strategic success isn't the entire story, however. First Chronicles 5:21 lists the considerable spoils they took. The verse concludes, "For many fell down slain, because the war was of God. And they dwelt in their place until the captivity."

The account encompasses three crucial elements: a problem, a prayer, and God's providence. The first two are simple enough. The problem, of course, was the reversal during the battle. The prayer describes their plea in the middle of the fighting.

Providence is a theological term. It describes God's divine attributes by which he preserves and governs all things according to his will. When the Scripture makes the simple statement that the war was of God, it means that he brought both sides to this particular battle at this particular time with this particular end in mind. This outcome was determined from eternity.

This raises significant questions regarding prayer and God's previously ordained will. Was the three tribes' near loss an illusion? Could they have leaned back against a grove of trees and watched the Lord go to work because their win was in the bag?

Faith doesn't work that way. First, God doesn't show us the big picture while we're in it. This episode is a case in point. He knew the battle and its ending long before it began, but the warriors did not. They had to fight.

Second, God had promised that the Conquest would be just that—a conquest. By design, they had to fight for their reward. Nor would God's people win the land overnight. Otherwise, he said, wild beasts would overrun Canaan and they would lose their inheritance to natural attrition (Deuteronomy 7:22-23). Because the Conquest involved real fighting, it also posed real dangers. The men were in dire straits. Their test of faith was a real one.

Third, God honors prayer. We must never forget this. The fighters cried out for his help, and he answered. The event was significant enough for the compilers of the Chronicles to record it. In doing this, they demonstrated a well-known New Testament principle, that God shows his strength in our weakness. The principle is easy to talk about but harder to carry out. In our individualistic culture, we like to solve our own problems. God works most effectively, however, when we have nothing to give.

In the end, this narrative offers us hope. It doesn't rise from a guaranteed formula that says if we pray hard enough, God is obligated to answer our prayer. If that were the case, we would be right back in dependency on our own faith. Further, we would have to throw out the concept of providence.

Our hope lies in our relationship to our God. He loves our prayers, even when they're the surprised exclamations following a battlefield reversal or the solitary nighttime pleas from a cancer victim. In prayer, the mortal calls to the eternal and says, "I can't do this. I need you."

We can't understand all the intricacies of the way God arranges problems, prayer, and providence, but we don't have to. He understands, and that's what counts. We can pray in good faith in any battle, whether it's against Canaanites, cancer, or anything in between.

Journal

When I pray for my crucial issue, how do I approach God in my prayer? How do I know he hears me? How do I change after my time with God?

_____

_____

_____

_____

_____

_____

_____

_____

_____

_____

_____

_____

_____

_____

Saturday, April 12

Four and a Half Months after Discovery

Cleo's Journey

Erastus stayed at Corinth, but Trophimus I have left at Miletum sick.
Do your best to come before winter. Eubulus greets you, with Pudens,
Linus, and Claudia, as well as all the brothers and sisters.
—2 Timothy 4:20-21

Why does God choose to take some while he lets others live?

Marie and I have been struggling with that question during the last couple days, after we heard the news that one of my fellow employees, a sister in Christ, has inoperable cancer—acute melanoma. Cleo and her husband, Norm, received the news from the Cleveland Clinic in March, a few days after Cleo fell ill to violent headaches and illness in the middle of a Florida vacation.

Marie and I have a visceral connection to Norm and Cleo. Marie's cancer is stage four, but it is treatable. Cleo has no hope for surgery or other treatment. The tumors on her brain and in her lungs are going to kill her. She has only weeks to live. From my perspective of measuring history, Cleo and Norm's ordeal came to light in the middle of ours. It was discovered a few months after our trial began and some months before our hoped-for end. Theirs will be a short and vicious fight with a predetermined end.

I learned about Cleo on Wednesday, when a mutual friend shared the news with me. I told Marie about it over supper before she left for her ladies' Bible study. While Marie was gone, I couldn't help comparing my situation to Norm's and wondering, with more than a little guilt over my self-centeredness, why he will be widowed soon while I will be able to enjoy my wife's continued presence. Yes, I still face the real possibility of such an occurrence, but for Norm it's a certainty. I marvel that I should be so blessed.

When Marie and I went to bed later that evening, she told me she had shared the same thoughts with the women from the church during their prayer time. Why should one lose her life while God permits another to go on?

Marie's response gave me some comfort. I'm not the only one asking. The questions arise naturally. Ultimately, though, we have to leave the answers in our God's hands, knowing that he determines our life spans on earth. Miraculous healing isn't an on-demand outcome.

Paul the apostle underscored this point at the end of his second letter to Timothy. When Paul wrote this letter, he was in prison awaiting execution for preaching the gospel. Now that he was measuring his life in months, things that once were less consequential became urgent. Three concerns come to the top in the closing verses of the book: the reality of sickness, the urgency of human contact, and the importance of relationships built on faith.

Paul dealt with the reality of sickness first. "Trophimus," he wrote, "I have left at Miletum sick" (2 Timothy 4:20). This is an unusual statement coming from one who once touched handkerchiefs and sent them away with healing power (Acts 19:12). Yet he understood that God does not necessarily desire to heal us in every circumstance. Sometimes the way we face suffering speaks more eloquently about our faith than the way we boast in wholeness.

Second, friendly human contact became a matter of crucial importance to Paul. This was the second time in the same letter he told his close younger friend to come. In 2 Timothy 4:9, he told Timothy to be diligent to come quickly, but here he became specific. "Do your best to come before winter" (2 Timothy 4:21). As great as Paul was, he needed the encouragement his son in the faith would be able to give him.

Finally, even in these last words, Paul exuded faith and optimism. Instead of pining over his impending death, he involved Timothy in what might be construed as small talk: "Eubulus greets you, and Pudens, Linus, and Claudia, as well as all the brethren." In this context, this kind of talk was anything but small, however. In the closing hours of Paul's life, those friendships were the most important thing he had because he knew they all would be beside him in their prayers to the end.

Norm and Cleo are there now. Their blog is called "Cleo's Journey," and it encapsulates their faith journey together, from Norm's missionary work in Brazil, Cleo's native country, to Cleo's ministry in Uberlandia, to Norm and Cleo's current works in the pastorate and jailhouse ministry for women.

Like Paul, they celebrate the past and hold on to the immediate. Cleo hopes to live long enough to see her grandchild, who is due in April. They treasure the tributes so many have posted on their blog site. And they continue to walk in faith as they look their last and most serious enemy in the eye.

Not many of us have the chance to face our own demise, and even fewer in such a dramatic way as Cleo and Norm. Like Paul's, their journey's end will be as courageous. They too have turned personal tragedy into an opportunity to share their faith. At the head of Cleo and Norm's site this magnificent statement appears: "God will get us through—not somehow, but triumphantly."

Author's note:

Marie died unexpectedly from complications of her cancer on April 24, 2003.
Cleo joined her in heaven on May 22.

Journal

What unexpected turns of events have occurred since this issue has come into my life? How has my faith helped me to face the issue?

_____

_____

_____

_____

_____

_____

_____

_____

_____

_____

_____

_____

Part 2

Grief and Hope

Sunday, April 27

Five Months after Discovery

Home-Going Faith

For I am already being poured out as a drink offering, and the time of my departure is at hand. I have fought a good fight, I have finished my course, I have kept the faith. Henceforth there is laid up for me a crown of righteousness, which the Lord, the righteous judge, shall give me at that day, and not to me only, but to all those who love his appearing.
—2 Timothy 4:6-8

I'm sitting at home on this Sunday morning, trying to collect my thoughts. Skipping church is not something I make a habit of doing, because I love my people, and I love God's command to assemble. But for two and a half days, I've been entertaining visitors and well-wishers, and I need time to think and grieve. It's the first chance I've had to be alone since my wife's passing.

Statistically, Marie was beating her cancer. Extrapolations on the cancer indices forecast that she would make a full recovery in a few months. But the future is never certain. On Tuesday she developed difficulty breathing and began to run a fever. Fearing infection, we took her to the emergency room, where they found fluid on her right lung. The fluid itself wasn't serious, but it was a situation they had to address. The hospital admitted her and scheduled a shunt to be placed on Thursday morning. They told us the procedure was nearly as straightforward as doing an IV. But when the technicians sat her up, a blood clot lodged in her pulmonary artery and sent her into cardiac arrest. She flat-lined three times, and in the end, they had to let her go.

Over the following few days, as we fitted the pieces together, we discovered what Marie understood already. She knew she would not survive the hospital visit.

This is what we know. Marie's mother was with her Wednesday morning when a chaplain visited Marie's room. He asked Marie if she knew the Lord, and she gave an articulate and ready testimony regarding her faith. The chaplain turned to her mother and said, "I guess we don't have to worry about this one."

I visited her that evening after work, and she was radiant. Her words to me—which I didn't yet understand would be her last—were full of the grace that typified her life. I'll never forget the love in her smile.

Then on Thursday she was gone.

The next day, a family friend related what Marie told her in confidence earlier in the week—the puzzle piece that let us know Marie was aware of her appointment with eternity. In words that were cryptic at the time, Marie mentioned a mutual promise they had made and told her friend to remember it for her.

"You'll be there too," the friend said.

Marie knew she wouldn't.

She displayed more than bravado in her last days. She exuded joy. What gives a person the ability to face death with such confidence?

Obviously it's faith, but what kind of faith? It's not the psyched-up faith that amounts to nothing more than meringue pie topping—more foam than substance. Those who see this kind of faith as the norm fail to understand the difference between our own subjective feelings and objective truth—what the Bible often calls "the faith." Without the latter, the former is worthless. My subjective faith, as important as it is, exists only in the present tense. It's what I have at any particular moment, and it's as mercurial as day and night temperatures in the desert.

The faith is something both bigger and more stable. We see it in the Apostle Paul's valedictory address when he wrote his last words to his friend and protégé, young Timothy, shortly before his martyrdom.

> For I am already being poured out like a drink offering, and the time has come for my departure. I have fought the good fight, I have finished the race, I have kept the faith. Now there is in store for me the crown of righteousness which the Lord, the righteous Judge, will award to me in that day—and not only to me, but also to all who have longed for his appearing (2 Timothy 4:6-8).

These words encompass Paul's past, present, and future. It's his expression of his faith in three tenses. He began with his present situation. His death was inevitable and would occur any day. Yet he didn't pen these words in despair. He wrote in the confidence that grew from what he knew was objectively true for all time.

Concerning the past, Paul said, "I have fought the good fight, I have finished the race, I have kept the faith."

His future was just as certain. "Henceforth there is laid up for me a crown of righteousness, which the Lord, the righteous judge, shall give me at that day, and not to me only, but to all those who love his appearing."

He could assert these things with such conviction because he understood the relationship between the two kinds of faith. His own subjective faith lay on the firm foundation of God's promises and not the other way around. He knew his Lord was faithful above anyone or anything else. He honestly could say concerning himself, "Wretched man that I am!" (Romans 7:24), but trust his destiny to the God who was eternally faithful when his life was about to come to its end.

Marie expressed similar misgivings at times. She often told me she thought others' outward expressions of faith were much more sincere than her own. By her reckoning her own faith was superficial. But those were her lean times, when she pressed forward despite her feelings. They were the times when the Lord stretched her limits and prepared her for her final task.

In the end, His work was good. A note that was inserted into one of the sympathy cards I received mentioned an attendant who assisted during the last frantic moments when the staff tried to revive Marie. This person was a believer as well and risked a breach of confidence to give us word that would cause our grieving hearts to soar.

He prayed for her as the Lord took her home.

Journal

In my time of extreme loss, where am I going to find comfort?

_____

_____

_____

_____

_____

_____

_____

_____

_____

_____

_____

_____

_____

Wednesday, June 18

Two Months after Passing

Good Grief

Sorrow is better than laughter, for the heart is made better by a sad countenance.

—Ecclesiastes 7:3

My best friend shared a wise proverb with me the other day. Life, he said, is a cruel taskmaster. She gives the tests first and then teaches the lessons.

We all face the taskmaster at one time or another. My call came when the Lord took my wife home just before our twenty-fifth anniversary.

Twenty-five years seems like a long time on the one hand. How often do we commit ourselves to a single track for a quarter of a century? I know of people who have filled the same position at their jobs for that long, but I don't think too many planned it. Marriage, on the other hand, is a once-for-all commitment to love, protect, and cherish—to have and to hold, for better or worse, for richer or poorer, in sickness and in health . . .

And then, when death does part us, to let our loved one go.

With only memories to fill my mind where the woman I loved once filled my arms, twenty-five years is too short a time. One person with uncommon understanding asked me a couple weeks after Marie died, "Genesis tells us that the husband and wife become one. What happens when that part of us is no longer there?" It was a million-dollar question, and I told her I would ponder it. There's enough to it that I could think about it for the rest of my life.

On the one hand, I hate the grief. My taskmaster pummels me. The beating saps me emotionally and physically. It puts me in a dark and lonely place and leaves my family wondering why I can't rejoin them in the joy of daily life.

Yet as hard as it is, I'm beginning to see that grief is a gift from God. It makes me run into his eternal arms, crying with childlike ease. My wife's premature death is helping me to know the comfort that comes from God alone, and that is shaping me into his image. He is a great God who can employ the curse that came from Adam's sin to teach his people the meaning of grace.

That brings me back to my best friend. He lost his only child, so he knows grief well. We view life from different perspectives, however. He doesn't yet know the one true God, and while he grieves with me, he sees life only as the taskmaster—cruel and impersonal. I know the personal God who wounds but also binds the wound and who loves me more profoundly than I have the capacity to imagine.

Though my friend and I approach life from opposite poles, we walk a common path. We both understand that as it breaks us, grief lays down priceless life lessons if we let it. Since we're all sons of fallen Adam, the lessons are as universal as the sin that brought death into the world. The lesson at the heart of the matter is subtler and crucially more important. If we miss it, we've missed the whole thing.

I've invited an older and much wiser man to accompany me in a tour of the lesson. He walked the same path and in the end did see the deep lesson at the heart of the matter. His name is Solomon, the third and last king of united Israel.

His reflections come from his most experimental work, the book of Ecclesiastes. As the shrewdest and most powerful man in his day, he amassed every luxury imaginable, only to find cobwebs at the bottom of his golden pot. Ecclesiastes is an account of this man's obsession with the question, "Why do we cling to life as a matter of life or death?" To find out, he indulged himself with every form of entertainment, from intellectual pursuits to entrepreneurial endeavors, from mirth to sex to alcohol. He discovered that life alone may be good for a few laughs, but by itself it remains empty. The qualities that make life mean something have to come from something deeper.

Solomon had a gift for gritty observation. He knew how to fill a volume with a few poetic lines. Here, along with a few things I've managed to glean about grief, life, and living, are Solomon's observations from Ecclesiastes. The master has the last say, since he said it so much better than I ever could.

First, it's okay to cry. Solomon wrote:

> The heart of the wise is in the house of mourning,
> But the heart of fools is in the house of mirth.
>
> —Ecclesiastes 7:4

Second, crying will come at the weirdest moments. Don't be embarrassed to let it come. Venting your emotion not only will help you, but also may encourage others to weep when they need to do so.

> To every thing there is a season,
> And a time to every purpose under the heaven . . .
> A time to weep,
> And a time to laugh;
> A time to mourn,
> And a time to dance . . .
>
> —Ecclesiastes 3:1, 4

Third, time does not heal all wounds. Some follow us through the grave and into eternity. It's no accident that the Scripture says that God himself will wipe away all tears from his saints' eyes. He saves the deepest wounds for his personal touch.

> I have seen the travail, which God has given to the sons of
>   men to be exercised in it.
> He has made everything beautiful in his time.
> Also he has set the world in their hearts, so that no man can
>   find out the work that God makes from the beginning
>   to the end.
>
> —Ecclesiastes 3:10-11

Fourth, when you have cause for real grief, you learn who your real friends are.

> Two are better than one,
> Because they have a good reward for their labor.
> For if they fall, the one will lift up his fellow;

> But woe to him that is alone when he falls;
> For he has no one to help him up.
>
> —Ecclesiastes 4:9-10

Fifth, when you have cause for real grief, you learn who your real friends aren't.

Corollary: I'm sure there's a jury out there who will acquit me when I throttle the next person who says, "God doesn't give you more than you can handle."

> The words of a wise man's mouth are gracious;
> But the lips of a fool will swallow himself.
> The beginning of the words of his mouth is foolishness,
> And the end of his talk is raving madness.
>
> —Ecclesiastes 10:12-13).

Sixth, memories are more important than things. It's not the big stuff but the daily routines that bear our loved-ones' fingerprints.

Corollary: Don't be afraid to share those memories or mementos with others when they want to grieve with you. It will allow them to share your grief, and it will go a long way toward making you a real friend when someone else needs one.

> There is a severe evil that I have seen under the sun,
> Namely, riches kept for their owners to their hurt.
> But those riches perish by bad fortune;
> A man begets a son, and there is nothing in his hand.
> As he came forth of his mother's womb,
> Naked shall he return to go as he came,
> And shall take nothing of his labor,
> Which he may carry away in his hand.
>
> —Ecclesiastes 5:13-15

Seventh, memories are built from love. Regrets grow like briars on careless words or choices. Whether we live with memories or regrets depends mostly on our own choices.

> If a man begets a hundred children, and lives many years, so that the days of his years are many, but his soul is not filled with good, or he has no burial, I say that a stillborn child is better than he.
>
> —Ecclesiastes 6:3

Eighth, grief is an invitation to trust in the God who loves us beyond the limits of our imagination. The trick is to learn to be content in the trusting.

> I know that, whatsoever God does,
> It shall be forever.
> Nothing can be added to it,
> Nor can anything be taken from it;
> And God does it that men should fear before him.
>
> —Ecclesiastes 3:14

Ninth, don't expect life to be fair.

> I have seen all things in the days of my vanity:
> There is a just man who perishes in his righteousness,
> And there is a wicked man who prolongs his life in his wickedness.
>
> —Ecclesiastes 7:15

Tenth, love those whom God brings into your life with all your might. Nothing else comes close in value.

> Live joyfully with the wife whom you love all the days of your vain life, which he has given you under the sun, all the days of your vanity; for that is your portion in this life, and in your labor that you take under the sun.
>
> —Ecclesiastes 9:9

Finally, be quick to reconcile your grievances, because the alternative might be heinous.

> Wisdom strengthens the wise
> More than ten rulers of the city.
> For there is not a just man upon earth who does good,
> And does not sin.
> Also do not take all the words you hear too seriously,
> Lest you hear your servant curse you.
>
> —Ecclesiastes 7:19-21

Those are some of the lessons I've picked up along the way. I can't say that I've arrived. To borrow a metaphor from Deuteronomy, the sky looks like brass. As often as not, I've prayed at the ceiling, and sometimes I've wondered if God was even real. More than once I've considered abandoning my Christian beliefs altogether.

My pants are torn, my knees are bloody, and my hands are chafed. Yet the Lord in his infinite grace picks me up again, brushes me off, and holds me in his ever-loving arms.

And this brings us to the heart of the matter. Simply stated, it's the possession of God. Solomon found him at the end. The last thing he wrote in his journal was this:

> Let us hear the conclusion of the whole matter: Fear God, and keep his commandments: for this is the whole duty of man. For God shall bring every work into judgment, with every secret thing, whether it is good or evil.
>
> —Ecclesiastes 12:13-14

We serve a sovereign God whose grace is immeasurable. It's not our hand that holds his but his hand that holds us.

Journal

What have I found—either good or bad—in grief? How am I reacting right now to my grief? What good thing can grow from my grief?

_____

_____

_____

_____

_____

_____

_____

_____

_____

_____

_____

_____

_____

_____

Commentary:

Avoiding the Humpty Dumpty Syndrome

Speaking Comfort to the Broken Without Trying to Reassemble the Pieces

Avoiding the Humpty Dumpty Syndrome

Speaking Comfort to the Broken Without Trying to Reassemble the Pieces

Grief is not so much a return trip to normalcy as a settlement in brokenness. When someone loses a loved one, part of that person dies as well. God created us to experience unending intimate relationships, and an intimacy that was never created to be destroyed finds itself torn in two by death. When I grieved Marie's loss, these issues came to the foreground in my thinking.

1. *Don't* try to make the person better. "Better" describes how we feel after we shake the flu. Grief doesn't get better. It will subside over time, sometimes waning and sometimes waxing, but its presence will remain.

2. *Do* recognize that the survivor will be forever changed. His or her life will move on, but it cannot go back. Part of the grief cycle is bound in the reality of a lost future as well as a past.

3. *Don't* say the departed one has gone to a better place. The term "better place" is a euphemism that could mean anything from materialistic nonexistence to nirvana. If you know the departed person shared the faith, say so. Otherwise, leave the subject alone.

4. *Do* feel free to share genuine hope. If you know the person is saved, acknowledge that he or she is with the Lord.

5. *Do* feel free to acknowledge the other person's loss. This shows that you care about the person.

6. *Do* be diligent to use correct doctrine. In one case a well-meaning friend told a father's grieving children, "God was lonely and needed another angel." Not only is this bad theology, but it also sent a message to the kids that God is selfish and takes what he wants without regard to people's feelings.

7. *Don't* be afraid to say you don't understand. If you haven't gone through the ordeal, you cannot understand. Our shared faith doesn't require us to know all the answers as much as it asks us to speak words of comfort. A word of sympathy spoken in love to a grieving person is more valuable than a truckload of inflated platitudes.

8. *Do* take the time to listen. Some of the most sincere comfort I received after my wife's death came from people who did no more than let me talk.

9. *Don't* try to teach lessons. Healing is not a highway to wholeness. It's a back road filled with ruts and potholes. If we act like we're in a hurry for grieving person to learn something, the effort ultimately wounds more deeply.

10. *Do* give the person space if he or she needs it. The need for distance is not a reflection on you. It is a product of the pain in the grieving person.

11. *Don't* go fishing. Grieving people need sympathy, not a lot of probing questions.

12. *Do* give mourners time to grieve and heal. Counselors tell us that a normal recovery time can take up to two to three years.

Sermon:

An Exposition of Psalm 44

A Sermon in Three Parts

Delivered to Community Baptist Church of
Tallmadge
Tallmadge, Ohio
November 20, 27 and December 4, 2011

Sermon: Psalm 44, Part 1
Mud Wrestling with God

Delivered to Community Baptist Church of Tallmadge
Tallmadge, Ohio
November 20, 2011

During the past week, two crises occurred among people who were either distantly or closely related to me. The first happened early in the week when a seventeen-year-old high school student from our area committed suicide. I did not know him, but his mother works at the university where I work. His funeral took place at the college chapel, and I witnessed the shock and grief in the crowd of high school students who came to pay their respects.

The second incident involved a married couple Patty and I both consider to be our best friends. Matt graduated from the seminary last year and recently accepted the call to pastor a small country church. We talked on the phone a couple nights ago, and Matt told me that last weekend a gang of juveniles burglarized his church. The church had been collecting donations for Franklin Graham's Samaritan's Purse Ministry, and the kids had put a lot of work into the project. The punks who broke into the building pilfered the cash from the Shoebox donations, tore up the boxes and gifts, stole a church cell phone, and even took cheese and beverages from the refrigerator. Matt told me the church is traumatized.

Have you ever been in a life situation that challenged everything you thought you knew about God and his ways? If you've lived any length of time at all, you have. Let me ask you this: If you experienced the situation as a Christian, how were you *allowed* to approach your personal crisis in the Christian culture in which you lived? How did your Christian brothers and sisters expect you to face your problem? I'm going to guess it was within a framework that looked something like this:

- You were allowed to acknowledge your grief, but you were expected to testify to the Lord's comfort within the grief at the same time.
- You were not allowed to admit any feelings of hopelessness. Those sentiments were out of bounds.
- You were not allowed to admit that you felt any anger toward God.
- You were expected to be confident that God would bring good through this situation. I call this the Romans 8:28 fast track.
- You had to show evidence that you were getting through the situation in a definite, positive, and visible way, because, after all, grief is foreign to the modern Christian culture, and getting over it is a mark of maturity.

Here's a quote from a recent *Christianity Today* article.

> We live in a culture that tries to avoid grief. We've discarded many of the cultural indicators of mourning: Widows don't wear black for a year; mothers who lose their children no longer cut their hair; we've given up on sackcloth and ashes . . . Christians have participated in this denial. Mortality and grief are rarely mentioned from the pulpit. Many churches have moved their graveyards from the center of town to the suburbs so we don't have to be reminded of death as we walk into the sanctuary on Sunday mornings.[1]

Don't we all know this? About a week before the end of spring quarter last year, at the seminary where I am a student, one of the graduating seniors lost her husband to a heart attack. He was in his early fifties and was apparently in good health. When the time came for the funeral, she told her friends not to wear black. The funeral was going to be a time for celebration and not mourning.

Why do we deny ourselves the opportunities to mourn?

I believe it's because we don't know what else to do. Mourning involves asking questions, and really spiritual people shouldn't have to question their faith. While we hemorrhage on the inside, we think to ourselves, *If I can just make myself believe my own words, maybe the bleeding will stop.*

Psalm 44 and Mourning

Psalm 44 is a psalm of mourning, a lament. One commentator describes the public psalms of lament as, "those which can be singled out from the description in I Sam. 7 of what was done and said as the Philistines oppressed the Israelites and the latter 'gathered together to Mizpah, and drew water, and poured it out before the LORD, and fasted on that day, and said there, We have sinned against the LORD.'"[2]

We typically avoid the laments. After all, they're so down, and we fear that if we study them, we may jinx the cosmic powers and bring bad things upon ourselves. I am convinced, however, that a relationship with the laments in Scripture is necessary for a healthy Christian life. This fact may come as a surprise to many, but the Psalms contain a greater number of laments than praises. Life is messy, and the Psalms reflect that messiness. When our personal experiences drag us into the mud pit, however, we find God is right there with us. It's okay to mud wrestle with God. In the case of Psalm 44, the wrestling comes in the form of mourning.

Today we begin a three-part series on Psalm 44. This week I want to look at Psalm 44 from the psalmist's perspective. What was he thinking? How did he set up his case? Next week we will discuss the theology and psychology in the psalm and look at its relationship to our understanding of God's work in our lives. Finally we'll finish the psalm and consider a broad range of applications.

Title Transcription

The transcription at the head of the psalm reads, "Of the sons of Korah. A Maskil."

Korah was one of the children of Israel who left Egypt in the Exodus. He was a descendant of Levi, which meant his occupation was in the priestly service. Korah's lineage put him in the group who serviced of the holy implements within the tabernacle (Ex. 6:24; Num. 3:27-32, 4:1-15). He occupied a very privileged position. He became famous—or infamous—for his uprising in Numbers 16, when he instigated open rebellion against God's appointed priests. Because his rebellion was so severe, God judged him and his 250 partners directly. The earth opened up, took Korah and his partners alive to the grave, and then closed behind them. Korah's children, however, refused to take place in the uprising and were spared (Num. 26:10-11). But that's not the end of their story. Korah's children became noted for their piety and devotion to God, a character trait that followed them for centuries in Old Testament Israelite history.

The psalm is a maskil. Rabbinic literature from the tenth century CE on understands a maskil to be a scholar, and their writings came to be known as maskils. Therefore when the ancient Hebrew readers saw this title, they would have known they were about to read a thoughtful work from one of the most pious groups in their national history. They would know to expect something deep and philosophical.

Verses 1-3: Historical prologue

> We have heard with our ears, O God,
> Our fathers have told us,
> The work you did in their days,
> In the times of old.
> It was you who drove out the nations with your
> hand, and planted them;
> You broke the peoples and cast them out.
> For they did not possess the land by their own
> sword,
> Nor did their arm save them:
> But your right hand, your arm, and the light of
> your presence,
> Because you showed them favor.

The first part of the psalm highlights Israel's history during the Conquest, when the second free generation went in and took the land of Canaan, as God had promised Abraham. I want you to notice three things about these verses:

- Everything in this psalm will stand on the foundation the psalmist lays in these verses. The psalm is grounded in God's work in history. The Exodus under Moses and the Conquest under Joshua gave the nation their sense of identity as God's people because of God's unprecedented work on his covenant people's behalf. This section has six references to the words *you* or *your*, where the psalmist acknowledges God for his work on the nation's behalf.

- Notice verse 1. The history was ancient, even to the Israelites during this time. This opening and other clues let us know that Psalm 44 is a late psalm. We'll address this point again when we develop the applications.

- Compare the first half of verse 3 with the rest of the section. The psalmist makes a deliberate negative statement: "not . . . by their own sword, / Nor did their arm save them." Then he goes back to his positive statement of faith. This positive-negative-positive triplet forms a pattern that he will repeat two more times. Not only did God work, but he worked distinctly apart from any human help.

Verses 4-8: The Psalmist's Present Faith Stand

> You are my King, O God:
> Command victories for Jacob.
> Through you we will crush our enemies:
> Through your name we will trample those who
> rise up against us.
> For I will not trust in my bow,
> Nor will my sword save me.
> But you have saved us from our enemies,
> And you have put those who hated us to shame.
> In God we boast all day long,
> We will praise your name forever. Selah

This section builds on the historical foundation in the first three verses. Just like the ancients who trusted the LORD and saw their trust rewarded in his great works on their behalf, the psalmist takes pains to declare his faith in the same bold terms. The positive-negative-positive cycle occurs again: "[Positive] Through you . . . Through your name . . . [Negative] I will not trust in my bow, / Nor will my sword save me. [Positive] But you have saved . . ." He makes his faith stand with a strong awareness that he is involved in the same history that his ancient ancestors occupied. His faith is the same as his ancient fathers' faith.

Further, just like verses 1-3, which were rich in acknowledgment for what God had done, this section contains another seven references to *you*, *your*, or *God* to acknowledge the LORD's works. The psalmist declares in no uncertain terms that he trusts his God to continue to work in the present time, just as his ancestors had in the past.

Verses 9-19: The Psalmist's Faith Crisis

Then the writer drops the bomb. Verses 9-16 contain this message:

> But you have cast us off,
> And put us to shame;
> You do not go out with our armies.
> You make us turn back from the enemy:
> Those who hate us took plunder for themselves.
> You have given us like sheep for slaughter;
> And have scattered us among the nations.
> You sell your people for nothing,
> And become no richer by their price.
> You make us a reproach to our neighbors,
> A mockery and scorn to those around us.
> You make us a joke among the nations,
> A shaking of the head among the people.
> My confusion is continually before me,
> And the shame of my face has covered me.
> Because of the voice of the one who taunts and mocks;
> Because of the enemy and avenger.

The writer's words are calculated to cut. They leave no ambiguity regarding his aggravation with his God. Like the verses before, this section attributes cause to God. It holds seven references to *you*, this time in reference to the damage. In the writer's mind, God was as responsible for his people's present defeat as he was for their past success.

If we're paying attention, these lines make us shrink in horror. We want to tell the psalmist, "You can't talk to *God* like this. After all, he's God, and this is supposed to be a prayer. What is he going to *think*?"

That's a good question. Let's consider it for a few moments. First, these are difficult words. We won't deny that. But whatever God might have thought about them when they first filled the parchment, he brought them into the Bible. The Holy Spirit directed them to become part of Israel's body of worship hymns. For that reason alone, we need to pay attention to them.

Second, they're there for more than just shock value. This psalm is a carefully crafted hymn, not a rotten tomato hurled against a wall. It represents the psalmist's honest thoughts, and they have been distilled with great care. He's hurting. He's in moral limbo, and he has serious questions about his God's faithfulness. He doesn't have any answers, and he's mourning out loud.

Finally, let's think the issue through. Do we really think the psalmist could have kept God from being offended if he had held his thoughts in? In another psalm David wrote:

> You know my sitting and my rising,
> You understand my thought from afar . . .
> For there is not a word on my tongue, O LORD,
> But that you know it already.
>
> —Psalm 139:2, 4

Psalm 139 is a psalm we love to read when everything is peaceful around us. It's a comfort psalm. Yes, he knows us when the kids are asleep and we're curled up on the couch, sipping chamomile tea. But the words apply equally to the times when we're in moral crisis. He knows us when we are trying to process the news that our Christmas tree caught fire and destroyed the house while we were away. He knows us equally when we're up all night pacing the floor and wondering where we're going to find the money to buy baby formula. Not only does he know the words we say, but he also knows the thoughts in our heads before we think them—whether they're peaceful or agitated.

Since this is the case, do you think God is going to be offended when we offer up naked prayer in our grief? Yes, certain things do offend God, but wrestling with him over his ways is not one of them.

We'll close this message with Psalm 44:17-19. This section completes the final positive-negative-positive triplet in the psalm. After the searing pronouncement against the LORD (the initial positive component), the writer adds:

> All this is come upon us; yet have we not forgotten you,
> Neither have we dealt falsely in your covenant.
> Our heart has not turned back,
> Nor have our steps turned from your way,
> Though you have broken us in the place of jackals,
> And covered us with the shadow of death.

The negative component occurs in verses 17-18: " . . . we have not forgotten you; / Neither have we dealt falsely with your covenant. / Our heart has not turned back, / Nor have our steps turned from your way." The calculation here is incredible. In the first two sections of the psalm, the negative components minimized any human activity: " . . . not . . . their own sword, / Nor . . . their arm . . ." (v. 3) and " . . . not . . . my bow, / Nor . . . my sword . . ." (v. 6). But in verses 17-18, we see less of a negation of human activity than a backhanded way of affirming his people's innocence. We could paraphrase the verses, " . . . we have remembered you; / We have stayed true to your covenant. / Our heart has remained with you, / Our steps have stayed on your way . . . ." Finally, the self-affirmation is subtle, but it will turn out to be significant. Verse 19 comes back to the positive statement and reaffirms the devastation the LORD has thrust upon them. "You have broken us . . . And covered us with the shadow of death."

The closing comment on the shadow of death was more than just an illusion for the psalmist. Judah was threatened by war. Modern archaeological excavations have unearthed a whole culture of warfare in the psalmist's world. In the ninth century BCE, the Assyrians became the first nation to develop a professional army and to invent the practice of mass deportation. Their armies became brutal psychological war machines. If a city's leaders refused to surrender to the "peace" gesture, the generals staged gruesome and public tortures outside the city walls as a preview of what would await the city officials when the Assyrians took them to the next city. When they did break through the walls, they uprooted all the people and took them away. Their victims would never see their homeland again.

The enemy wasn't satisfied just to win the battle. They turned the battlefields into killing fields. Ultimately Assyria was responsible for the deportation of the ten tribes of Israel in 722 BCE (2 Kings 17). A little over two hundred years later, Babylon adopted the same methods and did the same to Judah (2 Kings 24-25). The psalmist wrote during this time, when the Babylonian armies were preparing to sack Jerusalem.

Application

We're going to leave the poor sons of Korah here in the middle of the killing fields. We'll wait until the end of the psalm to draw an extended list of applications, although I do want to mention one reality today. Every one of us will experience times when God's purpose and character are hidden from us. This is not a contingency. It's a certainty. When it occurs, you will find certain things to be true:

- Difficulties are not something twenty-first-century Christians like to acknowledge. We like certainty and despise deviance from it. When we find ourselves under prolonged duress while the rest of the fellowship goes on with their lives, we may find ourselves distanced from the fellowship.
- You may discover that you not only grieve the event that is occurring, but you also find yourself angry with God for his absence during the event. On one hand, it's okay to admit that you're angry with God. Anger is part of grieving. It saturates the Psalms. On the other, the careful structure of this psalm hints at boundaries to our anger. We'll look at these closely next week when we look at the psalm's guiding principle. For now, suffice it to say that anger against God can be right or wrong. The way we approach God in the dark times will constitute the difference between praying as if we're writing hymns or throwing tomatoes.

Sermon: Psalm 44, Part 2
Theology at Ground Zero

Delivered to Community Baptist Church of Tallmadge
Tallmadge, Ohio
November 27, 2011

The title of the sermon today is "Theology at Ground Zero." When this psalm was written, the people of Judah were watching their nation capitulate before their enemy. The bomb was heading straight toward their laps, and all they could do was wait for the detonation to occur. Their theology was in crisis. They were in the midst of grief. We'll look at the middle section of the psalm and consider three themes:

- Theology and crisis
- Crisis and grief
- What happens when grief collides with theology

Theology in Crisis

If I were to ask whether the way you relate to God now differs from the way you did twenty years ago, most of us would say, "Of course it does. I know more about him, and I know him more deeply than I did before." This is the way it should be because it reflects normal Christian growth.

Now let me ask another question. When and how did this growth take place? The normal avenues for growth are clear from the Bible.

- We grow in our relationship with God through our interaction with each other in the fellowship.
- We grow as we look for ways to serve our fellow believers.
- We grow through our own personal prayer and Bible study. The more effort we put into any of these, the greater the benefits.
- Finally, like it or not, sometimes our relationship with God grows through crisis.

The psalmist's theology is straightforward. His basic theology—the way he relates to his God—comes from Deuteronomy.

> When the LORD your God brings you into the land that you are going to possess, and he drives out the nations before you—the Hittites, and the Girgashites, and the Amorites, and the Canaanites, and the Perizzites, and the Hivites, and the Jebusites, seven nations greater and mightier than you—and when the LORD your God delivers them before you, you must strike them and utterly destroy them. You will not make a covenant with them or show mercy to them . . . .
>
> —Deuteronomy 7:1-2

For the psalmist, theology meant keeping the house clean. This involved two things. First, they were to stay away from idols; God alone was their God. If the people kept their religion pure from outside pollution and maintained a strong devotion to their God, they were certain they would come out victorious. Second, they were to remember their identity, and identity is simple. They were the covenant people—the good guys—and everyone else was a bad guy. And the way to deal with the bad guys was either to convert them or drive them out. This theology defined their approach to battle and to life. In their minds, internal obedience and blessing lived in one-to-one correspondence with each other.

Their theology became even more entrenched with the construction of the temple. In Israel's middle history, both the throne of David the king and the temple that emerged from his efforts became perpetual entities. The temple-building project began when David shared his heart with Nathan the prophet: "See now, I dwell in a house of cedar, but the ark of God dwells behind curtains" (2 Sam. 7:2). Nathan told David to pursue his passion, but then he received a different word from the LORD that night. Using a play on words that exists both in the original language and in English, God said he would do two remarkable things for David's "house":

> When your days are complete and lie down with your fathers, I will set up your descendant after you, who shall proceed from you, and I will establish his kingdom. He will

build a *house* [i.e., temple] for my name, and I will establish the throne of his kingdom forever . . . But my mercy shall not depart away from him, as I took it from Saul, whom I drove away from before you. And your *house* [i.e., dynasty] and your kingdom shall be established forever after you: your throne will be established forever.

—2 Samuel 7:12-13, 15-16, emphasis added

When the LORD made his covenant with David, he changed the face of Old Testament theology. The law covenant under Moses was conditional. The people had to obey to be blessed. God's covenant with David was unconditional. God would establish the nation, the religion, and the dynasty under King David's name. They were to be everlasting entities, and the nation took these words to the bank. Their temple and their identity were invincible.

Now, however, the people were in dire straits. Internal evidence places this psalm near the end of Judah's existence as a nation, contemporaneously with Jeremiah the prophet, "during the last spasms of Judah's agony."[3]

The psalmist and his companions had done everything right, but the enemy stood before them like a wolf pack about to converge on a wounded deer. The nation was in trauma. No wonder the psalmist wrote:

> My confusion is continually before me,
> And the shame of my face has covered me.
> Because of the voice of the one who taunts and mocks;
> Because of the enemy and avenger.
>
> All this is come upon us; yet have we not forgotten you,
> Neither have we dealt falsely in your covenant.
> Our heart has not turned back,
> Nor have our steps turned from your way,
> Though you have broken us in the place of jackals,
> And covered us with the shadow of death.
>
> Verses 15-19

Crisis and Grief

The people, the temple, and their worship all were about to die. Of course, the ancient writer had no way of knowing this, but the crisis had put him in the middle of a grief cycle. Modern psychology has mapped out the grief cycle to include five stages. The following descriptions come from *Elisabeth Kübler-Ross,* a noted grief expert.

- Denial
- Anger
- Bargaining
- Depression
- Acceptance[4]

We call grief a cycle because the first three stages take us down to a nadir, or a low point. The depression stage, as bad as the term sounds, actually marks the turning point as the person begins a process of admission. Kübler-Ross describes depression as a period of acceptance with emotional attachment that comes before full acceptance. We go through the first steps until we finally come to full acceptance of what has happened. Let's see where these cycles enter the psalm.

- **Denial**: In a subtle way, the psalmist is still in denial. His statement of faith in verses 4 through 8 reflects this struggle. Theologically he puts up a brave front: "No matter what happens I'm still going to maintain my faith." Psychologically he appears to think, *This will go away; this will go away . . .*

- **Anger**: Do we see anger in this psalm? Absolutely. We could title verses 9 through 16, "The Anger Section." Look at the first lines of these verses:

  - Verse 9: But now you have rejected and humbled us . . .
  - Verse 10: You made us retreat before the enemy . . .
  - Verse 11: You gave us up to be devoured like sheep . . .
  - Verse 12: You sold your people for a pittance . . .

- **Bargaining**: Verses 17 through 26, which we read earlier, can be construed as "The Bargaining Section." Theologically, "Israel presents herself as being 'oppressed, distressed, miserable, in need of help' . . . This description is in itself aimed at getting the prayer heard: it is intended to rouse the compassion of Yahweh and make him help."[5] Psychologically, the psalmist is using this section to set up his case. In verse 17, he brokers his people's sincerity of heart:

"All this came upon us, though we had not forgotten you;
We had not been false to your covenant . . ."

In return, he hopes to regain God's good favor. Look at verses 23 through 24:

"Awake, LORD! Why do you sleep?
Rouse yourself! Do not reject us forever.
Why do you hide your face
and forget our misery and oppression?"

Do you see the bargaining? The psalmist says in effect, "We're good people, LORD. Please honor us as good members of your covenant."

- **Depression and Acceptance**: The last two stages of grief mark the turning point in the process as the grieving person comes to grip with reality. But we don't see acceptance of any kind in this psalm. It just isn't there. We are in the middle of unresolved anguish—at the very bottom of the grief cycle.

When Grief Collides with Theology

Now we come to the last section of the psalm, where we'll look more closely at the matter of application from the perspectives of psychology and theology. One modern writer observes that these verses show a "transition from psychology to theology."[6] He's right, but we don't want to place a wall between the two. Whether we do psychology or theology, we study under the lordship of Christ. The Psalms are not expressions of raw emotion. They are experience and emotion processed through the way we listen.

This is particularly true of this psalm. The anger section in verses 9 through 16 and the bargaining section in verses 17 through 24 are not just raw. While the writer may be in grief, he does not let his emotions run rampant. He processes them through the listening section. We see an important statement of this in verse 4:

> "You are my King, O God,
> Command victories for Jacob."

The Stated Meaning: Some modern versions translate this as a declarative statement—"You are my king and my God, who decrees victories for Jacob" (NIV)—but the imperative mood reflects the literal meaning of the verse. The psalmist is calling on the LORD to bring victory to Jacob. There are two shades of meaning in this verse. The first comes with the writer's statement, "Command victories for Jacob."

The logic is simple. God is King, and a king's job is to bring victory in battle. The psalmist's earthly king had failed. Babylon was about to crush Judah like a Mack truck rolling over a toy car. In response, then, the psalmist hearkens back to the theology in 1 Samuel 8, when Samuel warned against placing a man on the throne. God alone was to be the nation's king. The psalmist says in effect, "God, I count you as king even over my earthly ruler, and I have greater confidence that you will bring victory than even the man who occupies the throne." On the surface, therefore, the logic is simple:

> You are my real King
> Kings bring victory.
> Therefore, I want to see you bring victory.

The Deeper Meaning: But there is more to the meaning of this verse. Whether he realizes it or not, the psalmist bows to a guiding principle. The words, "You are my King, O God," do more than set up a platform for the psalmist's demands. They also place him under the King's authority. Because of that, he gives up the right to make categorical demands on his King. The anger section and the bargaining section, therefore, ultimately are guided by the psalmist's theology. His theology reins in his emotions.

How does he do this?

Both his anger and his bargaining fall under the boundaries of the statement, "You are my King." In each section, the writer makes an affirmation, but he refrains from taking his affirmation to its emotional extreme.

- In verses 9 through 16, the anger section:
  - o The writer attributes *cause* to God. Cause means, "You did this." *Cause* acknowledges God's sovereign control over his creation. The writer understood that both the blessings and the disasters were meted out by God.
  - o He does not attribute *blame* to God. Blame means, "This is your fault." Blame shifts the center of righteousness from God to myself. It says, "God, what you did was unfair to *me*." This doesn't happen in this text.

- In verses 17 through 22, the bargaining section:
  - o The writer recognizes his freedom to defend his moral case in God's presence, and he uses it. He and his compatriots have examined themselves, and they have found nothing in their hearts to betray their God. Their case for righteousness is both honest and humble.
  - o He does not elevate his own moral righteousness or try to leverage it against God to demand fair treatment. He pleads for mercy but never demands lenience.

What does this mean for us? It means two things.

On one hand, we are human. We have psyches. We have the right to bow under the psychological pressures God has created in us, and that includes the freedom to be angry with God. Nowhere does the Bible call us to forfeit our right to experience or acknowledge universal human emotions when we name the name of Christ.

The balancing truth is that we are redeemed. We have the charge to act responsibly before the God who has saved us. While our theology doesn't deny our emotions, it does govern them. Ultimately we have a responsibility before God to act in ways that glorify him. We'll explore this theme more deeply next week.

Sermon: Psalm 44, Part 3

Waiting for *Khesed*

Delivered to Community Baptist Church of Tallmadge
Tallmadge, Ohio
December 4, 2011

To help pay my tuition at Ashland Seminary, I work as a graduate assistant in the Seminary Writing Center. Students are encouraged to submit their papers to the center before they hand them into their professors so we can help them clean them up. Over the year and a half that I've been contributing to the job, I've found that my work falls into three levels.

- The first and most basic level has to do with the rules of spelling and grammar. These are hard and fast
- The second has to do with effective writing and expression—how the students might construct sentences or use phrases. Often this involves the difference between the spoken word and the written word. For example, a student might write, "She's about to argue for . . ." I will correct this to, "She is about to argue for . . ." Either version is acceptable grammatically, but academic writing does not like contractions. In other words, the rules for formal writing don't stand on the same level as the ones for grammar, but they're still very regular.
- The last area has to do with style. This is the most subjective of the three areas. Here I will say things like the following:
  - o "I think this way of phrasing this will be work better."
  - o "Let's rearrange this sentence so you explain the logical cause first and then discuss the effect."
  - o Or even, "I think this way of making your point would be more effective, but your way is all right. It's your choice."

Last week a friend with whom I had shared classes submitted a term paper for a class on the theology of suffering. The assignment was to recall a period of grief and walk the reader through it. The students were to chart the course of grief as it moved through their lives and discuss how their experience interacted with their personal theologies. My friend had lost her uncle and chose to write about that experience. He had been the father figure in her life and had died three weeks before. She wrote her paper in the middle of her grief crisis

I felt like I was on holy ground.

Her paper was so honest in the midst of pain that it became something too fragile to be tinkered with. I changed only the most necessary points in spelling, grammar, and writing conventions. In the few areas where I normally would have offered stylistic suggestions, I left it alone. It was just too sacred to alter.

Though she didn't realize it, my friend touched on all five sections of the grief cycle. She acknowledged her denial, anger, and bargaining, and at the end, she talked about the resolution she had begun to experience in the writing. Her words showed the first signs of depression and acceptance, the last two stages of the grief cycle. In other words, my friend wrote from a place that was very close to where we have been in our study of Psalm 44.

We will conclude the psalm today. We'll make some brief comments on the final two verses and then take the bulk of the sermon to bring in applications over the entire psalm. Let's read verses 25 through 26.

> "Our souls have sunk to the dust;
> Our bodies cling to the ground.
> Rise up, be our help;
> And redeem us because of your unfailing love."

Have you ever felt like you were brought down to the dust—like your body clung to the ground? I'm sure we all have when crises loomed and hope was beyond visibility. The psalm is like this. It ends in a whimper, without resolution, and without hope. We see only a plea: "Rise up, be our help; / And redeem us because of your unfailing love."

The last term, "unfailing love," comes from the Hebrew word, *khesed*. It's a word with a broad range of meanings. It carries the connotations, steadfast love, particular love, zealous love, mercy, pity, grace, or favor. For the Old Testament Hebrew, *khesed* described the very character of God. Here are some examples of the word in early Old Testament usage:

Exodus 15:13—After the Lord brought the Israelites across the Red Sea, Moses and the children of Israel sang a song that carried this line: "In your *khesed* you will lead the people you have redeemed. In your strength you will guide them to your holy abode."

Exodus 20:5-6—The delivery of the Ten Commandments on Mount Sinai: "You shall not bow down to [idols] or worship them; for I, the LORD your God, am a jealous God, visiting the children for the sin of the fathers to the third and fourth generation of those who hate me, but showing *khesed* to a thousand [generations] of those who love me and keep my commandments."

Exodus 34:6-7a—When God declared his glory to Moses while he was on the Mountain. This is a defining moment in God's revelation to his people: "And he passed in front of Moses, proclaiming, 'The LORD, the LORD, the compassionate and gracious God, slow to anger, abounding in *khesed* and faithfulness, maintaining *khesed* to thousands, and forgiving wickedness, rebellion and sin . . .'"

Joshua 2:12—When Rahab hid the two spies, she made this bargain with them: "Now then, please swear to me by the LORD that you will show *khesed* to my family, because I have shown *khesed* to you."

Psalm 23:6a—David's second-to-last statement: "Surely goodness and *khesed* will follow me all the days of my life."

But *khesed* hasn't followed the writer of Psalm 44. All the theology he thought he had all tied up with a bow has vanished. His only recourse is to pray. That's not a bad thing, however. Do you remember the national reaction on 9/11? No one went down to visit the reference section of his local library to find what theological point he had missed in his assumptions on national security and divine protection. We didn't want more facts. We fell to our knees in prayer, because we needed to know that God would still take us in his arms. We craved God's *khesed*.

Applications

The very fact that this psalm ends without resolution draws us to certain truths. Christians don't have all the answers, and sometimes we enter places that defy answers. That carries certain implications with it.

It should teach us to examine our Christian sensibilities. Does the counsel we offer the wounded sometimes seek to draw them into our own comfort zone instead of leading them to the God of comfort? What I mean is this: popular Christian culture has little understanding or tolerance for suffering. If you don't believe it, think about our worship songs and the proverbial Scripture passages we apply to those who are in grief. Do they actually have substance, or are they just aphorisms?

Here are several that we might be tempted to throw at this psalm:

"God works all things together for good"

True, he does, but that truth is first a head truth, and becomes a heart truth only later. When someone is in a place where hope is invisible, the Romans 8:28 fast track doesn't help at all.

Or we might pull out this Scripture:

"Behold, He who keeps Israel
Will neither slumber nor sleep."

—Psalm 121:4

Or we might quote the one that says, "I will never leave you nor forsake you." We likely found this verse in Hebrews 13:5, but its original context is from Deuteronomy 31:6 and 8.

Yet the psalmist in our psalm feels forsaken. He writes,

"Awake, Lord! Why do you sleep?
Rouse yourself! Do not reject us forever."

—Verse 23

Throwing verses like these at those who are grieving is like whipping them with the Word. A grieving person isn't looking for reasons. He or she is looking for comfort and understanding.

A subtler error is the belief that knowing God's plan is the same as knowing God. When we tell people, "Someday you'll understand," we offer them false hope. Not long ago, the host on a one-minute featured spot on a Christian radio station told about a business venture she and her husband had pursued several years before. During the business's planning period, they found steady success, and they concluded God was in the move. Then, without warning, God closed the door. They didn't understand why this had happened, and they prayed about the matter. Still they found no answer. Finally, years later they learned about a critical factor that they couldn't have known about during the planning stages. The factor would have challenged the success of their venture. Now they could see what they couldn't before, and they were glad God redirected their plans.

The speaker didn't divulge any of the details regarding what their proposed business was or how they found out the new information. For her the important part was the knowing. In a subtle way, she began to shift her faith from God to the way God reveals his will. The resolution did not come from trusting God but in knowing the details. By implication, the speaker told her listeners that if we wait long enough, God will show us the answer. This is never taught in Scripture.

What about the shot we take from our easy chairs, "God never gives you more than you can handle"? That retort deserves to be taken to the desert, shot dead, and left for the jackals. Would any of us be willing to go back to the psalmist's day and tell him, "You're only facing torture, deprivation, and the loss of your family, your worship, and your national identity. You can handle it." For the sons of Korah, God's absence alone was too much to handle. When God isn't there, what can we handle? If we must resort to apothegms, we should tell people, "God will never put us through anything *he* can't handle."

Perhaps the cruelest statement of all that we make to those who are grieving is, "There must be a reason for this. What did you do?" This has its roots in the "knowing" fallacy. It shares the presumption that resolution comes ultimately from our ability to understand, but it adds a twisted moral component. If we're experiencing difficulty, we must have done something to earn it. Once we come to understand what we've done to cause the difficulty, we can confess the sin and watch the difficulty go away.

This line of thought assumes that God rewards all good deeds and punishes all evil deeds. It ultimately creates a works-oriented sense of justification and destroys compassion. In the book of Job, this assumption drove Job's three friends into a feeding frenzy, leading them ultimately to lash out at him with vicious accusations (Job 22:1-11). We must not forget grace. If God drew a straight line from sin to judgment, we all would be dead.

Those are negative applications. On the positive side, God gives us a great deal of freedom:

- We have the freedom to mourn. I can't stress this too much, particularly in our modern Christian culture. We don't have to be happy all the time to be spiritual. In and of itself, sadness is not a reflection of spiritual failure.
- We have the right to wrestle with God over issues we don't understand. The psalmist wrote:

"Yet for your sake we face death all day long
We are considered as sheep to be slaughtered."
—Verse 22

This is wrestling.

- We have the right to recognize that life is ragged and doesn't always fit into neat little boxes. Our hope must lie in the fact that God is bigger than either life or the boxes.
- We have the freedom to be appalled before God. The psalmist freely declared,

"You have rejected us and brought us to dishonor . . .
You cause us to turn back from the adversary . . .
You give us as sheep to be eaten . . ."
—Verses 9a, 10a, 11a

- We have the freedom to recognize that our relationship with God is dynamic rather than static. It is not constrained by rigid and legalistic rules of cause and effect (vv. 17-19).

- We can recognize that when bad things happen to us, they don't necessarily reflect a one-to-one correspondence with our deeds (verses 20-21). Verses 20 through 21 also imply that we are allowed to weigh the secrets of our own hearts and take them before God. The fact that God knows the secrets of our hearts already (v. 21b) shows us that we're not going to surprise him. We can honestly pray to him even when our prayer is brutally honest (v. 15). Psalm 131 provides an excellent commentary on this point.

The freedom to examine ourselves comes with a caveat, however. We also have the responsibility to listen to what God may reveal to us about the secrets in our hearts. Let's review a couple verses:

> All this is come upon us; yet have we not forgotten you,
> Neither have we dealt falsely in your covenant.
> Our heart has not turned back,
> Nor have our steps turned from your way.
>
> —Verses 17-18).

We know that this psalm was a late work. Much of the psalm's language bears strong resemblance to that of Jeremiah during the Babylonian holocaust around 605-587 BCE, making this the period of the psalm. For more than a hundred years, the prophets had warned the wealthy in Israel and Judah about God's impending judgment against them for their entrenched disregard toward the poor and the justice due them. "The singer of Psalm 44 . . . had not been convinced by the oracles of the great prophets, from Amos and Hosea, Isaiah and Micah, or Jeremiah, his contemporary (Jer. 7:1-11) . . . The psalmist insists on the purity of the cult [i.e., the worship practice centered in the temple]. He is silent on the oppression of the poor."[7]

The psalmist studied his worship and found it to be pure, and it undoubtedly was. But the critical issue in later Israelite history involved the administration of justice, to which the religious elite had become blind. None of us is immune from spiritual blindness in one form or another. God can use calamity to awaken us to issues we don't know exist.

- We have the right to believe our suffering matters to God. The psalmists clearly believed this, or they wouldn't have written this psalm. This implies any number of things. I'll close with these.
  - o Our suffering matters to God because he cares about us. We don't earn extra favor from God because of our suffering. To the contrary, Christ's work on the cross has purchased complete and perfect standing before God. Our suffering does not gain points before God. It cannot make us more saved than we already are, and neither can it earn credits for us to pass on to anyone else. Nonetheless, it has value. In Philippians 3, Paul talks about knowing "the fellowship of [Christ's] sufferings, being conformed to His death" (Phil 3:10). When we suffer, we learn firsthand what Jesus went through, and that knowledge draws us into closer fellowship with him than all the good fortune in the world could.
  - o Also see Colossians 1:24, where Paul's suffering on behalf of the church fills in what is lacking in Christ's sufferings. The lack is not a theological one but a temporal one. The world can't see Christ in the flesh, but they can see him in us. Our suffering gives us the opportunity to show his sufferings to the lost in a very concrete way. When the world sees us suffering with grace, they have the opportunity to see Christ behind our suffering.
  - o Suffering causes us to look for a perfect eternity instead of just a better present. Romans 8:22 reads, "For we have been saved in hope, but hope that is seen is not hope, for why should someone hope for what he can see?" Hope that is seen—visible hope—is what takes place in history. Our unseen hope is eternal. We're on earth only for a lifetime. Even if it spans a hundred years, it's a breath compared to eternity. Therefore, if life were pitch perfect, what would make us long for eternity? Suffering redirects our attention

to the everlasting glory the Lord has promised to his children.

o   Some lessons—particularly those regarding the proof of our faith—are gained only in a crucible. We cannot know whether we're brave enough for the battle until we have endured the battle and have gained the scars that become the proof of our genuineness. We can look back on these and count them as treasures on Christ's behalf.

Finally, let's consider Paul's use of this psalm. In Romans 8:35, he wrote, "Who shall separate us from the love of Christ? Shall tribulation, distress, famine, persecution, nakedness, peril or sword?" Then he quoted Psalm 44:22. The Romans passage reads, "As it is written, 'For your sake we face death all day long; we are counted as sheep to be slaughtered.'"

The Christians in Rome knew suffering firsthand. When Paul wrote to the Roman Christians, he wasn't just looking for a handy verse to drop into his context. He had every drop of the lacerated bloodiness in Psalm 44 in mind. When we're going through hell on earth and we don't *feel* worthy of Christ's love, we must remember that this passage is quoted in the very context of Christ's love.

The purpose for Christ's suffering was not just to purchase our salvation. It was also to allow him to learn firsthand to empathize on our behalf so we never would have to face such things alone. The author of Hebrews writes, "To the degree that he himself suffered when he was tempted, he is able to help those who are being tempted" (Heb. 2:16-17). Therefore, when we find ourselves mired in grief, when the world judges us as abnormal, and when even the church's praise songs come across like taunts, we can know that our Lord Jesus Christ remains with us and loves us no less. He stands beside us and whispers, "I understand what you're going through. I've been there."

Monday, December 15

Eight Months after Passing

The Back Side of Grief

Now Moses kept the flock of Jethro his father-in-law, the priest of Midian, and he led the flock to the back side of the desert, and came to the mountain of God, to Horeb.

—Exodus 3:1

I'm facing a hurdle of sorts today. A twenty-fifth anniversary should be a joyful milestone. I'd just never anticipated spending the day alone.

It's been eight months since cancer claimed Marie's life. While grief takes the lead in its slow dance with my family and me, we mark off first holidays—Thanksgiving, Christmas, a birthday we can't celebrate. We're robbed of our wife, mother, and friend.

Our anniversary, however, is mine alone.

My Bible tells me we'll be together again someday—no longer as husband and wife but as the bride of Christ. Our joy will be complete in him. But trying to subsist on that promise alone is like being chained to the wall outside a banquet room. I hunger for Marie, and the aroma of a too-distant promise in a different relationship only makes the hunger that much more acute. To be honest, I don't like God's way of sharing. My mortal hasn't put on immortality. I want Marie to be mine, not his.

Yet the Lord has been gracious to grant me hope through strange means. After spending weeks trying to convince myself and everyone else that I was standing strong in my faith, I gave in to my anger. Alone in my canoe on the Black Fork River, I prayed, "Lord, you count a thousand years as a day. Why couldn't you give me another twenty-five with my wife?"

God is never in a hurry to answer mortal challenges, and I finished my trip without an answer. About a month later, however, I experienced a realization that bordered on an epiphany. It was almost as if God said to me, "If I had given you another twenty-five years with her, would you have grieved any less?" I began to accept the truth. If Marie had survived, she would have lived with unceasing pain. She was ready to go home, to settle into her heavenly Father's arms, and to have him wipe away her tears. Realizing her death was in God's time was my first step toward acceptance.

The second realization came when I contemplated the Scripture and rediscovered how the Lord uses people he breaks. The passage involved Moses, one of my heroes. If ever a man had his ticket to success yanked from his hand, it was he. Miraculously saved from an angry pharaoh's genocidal rage and adopted into the very household that tried to exterminate his people, he had every opportunity to rise above his heritage. He just thought he could control his destiny.

His intentions were noble. When he had grown to manhood, he chose the more difficult of two courses of action. Rather than resting in his adopted pedigree, he decided to identify with his enslaved people. (His courage is lauded in Hebrews 11:24-27.) All he had to do was to make his loyalty known to his fellow Hebrews.

His big chance came when he was forty years old. He saw an Egyptian slave master beating one of the Hebrew slaves. Checking to see that no one was around, he killed the slave master and buried him in the sand. After all, the man was a common enemy. Who would tell?

The cultural bridge between himself and his people turned out to be larger than he'd realized. The next day, Moses discovered that he'd become a double turncoat. His people refused to trust him, and the pharaoh sought to kill him. He fled the country, broken. He'd blown the one big chance life had given him and had become the classic washout. What would the Lord want with him now? He settled in Midian, where he obtained a commoner's job tending sheep, fully expecting to spend the rest of his life with a bunch of stupid animals that couldn't fend for themselves. The job occupied his attention until he was eighty.

Exodus 3 brought Moses to the west side of the desert. Since east was the forward direction in Hebrew culture, looking west meant one was looking backward. The literal translation is "the back side of the desert." There he encountered the angel of the Lord in a bush ablaze with fire but that refused to be consumed.

In this place, the Lord called Moses to go back to the pharaoh to demand his people's freedom. This time the Lord would go with him. Ultimately

Moses liberated an entire nation, leading his people across the Red Sea, overseeing the building of the tabernacle, and shepherding them for the next forty years in the desert. Interestingly, Moses' first eighty years occupy only two chapters of Exodus, the book that introduces him. His life as Israel's deliverer encompasses the rest of Exodus, as well as the books of Leviticus, Numbers, and Deuteronomy. He became the greatest deliverer in biblical history until Jesus Christ. But God could not call Moses to the task intended for him until he took him to the back side of the desert, where self and ego counted for nothing and where God's preparation counted for everything.

I've learned a similar lesson. If he has broken me, it's for a purpose. After I finish work today, I'll walk back to the gravesite to give Marie a carnation and an anniversary card. I'll probably cry while I'm there, but it won't be the hopeless despair I'd anticipated because God has given me hope. Sure, I know I'll see her again in heaven—but that's not what encourages me right now. The present-day truth has begun to make me believe my life will have purpose again.

The Lord calls from the back side of grief. There's work to be done.

Journal

As I consider how to return to a functioning life, what motivates me to move beyond my past and plan a future? When I find myself mired in despair, what small steps can I take to begin to climb out of it?

_____

_____

_____

_____

_____

_____

_____

_____

_____

_____

_____

Monday, July 19

A Year and Three Months after Passing

Or So They Say

So when this corruptible shall have put on incorruption and this mortal
shall have put on immortality, then the written saying will come to pass,
"Death is swallowed up in victory."

—1 Corinthians 15:54

They say bad things come in threes, but I'm not very interested in what people say—not when we must choose between popular opinion and Scripture, anyway. Even though I'm facing my third family death in a year and a half, I have to trust the Bible to be my authoritative guide in life matters. God's sovereign choice is more loving than anyone's fatalistic understanding of the events that have brought exquisite grief to me and my family.

Dad died a year and a half ago, on the same day Marie and I learned about her cancer. Five months later, Marie lost her life. Mom and I leaned on each other then, not only as mother and son but also as adults who shared common losses. Mom's health was failing, however, and the family knew she wouldn't be around much longer. She missed Dad. We began to estimate her remaining time in weeks.

People who love soon discover that it's a dangerous thing. The ones we love grow into us, and when they die, part of us dies with them. The ache reaches into our souls. Maybe my three-beat cycle has given my understanding a fresh perspective, or maybe I was just slow to learn the first or second times. At any rate, this third time, another truth has hit me at a gut level. Someday I'm going to join them.

This world isn't all there is. Down here we're mortal, and our days are numbered. Moses, who watched perhaps a million people die violent deaths during his ministry,[8] wrote in Psalm 90, "Teach us to number our days, that we may apply our hearts to wisdom." We're all headed the same direction, and Moses' call is a good one.

For those who know the Lord, our final end is filled with hope. Yet even with the truth that absence from the body is presence with the Lord, as the apostle Paul wrote in 2 Corinthians 5:6-8, the journey isn't any less painful. This was true with Mom. As age and disease pummeled her body, she struggled with fear of death. Until Christ returns, we see only this side, and no amount of come-on-in-the-water's-fine makes the jump any easier.

This is why Paul took so much space to write about the issue in 1 Corinthians 15. Our Lord Jesus Christ went there and came back. The proof lies in the Old Testament Scriptures that looked forward to his death, burial, and resurrection, and in the eyewitness testimonies from those who saw Jesus alive after he came back from the dead.

As we trust in him to bear our sin, we also trust him to carry us across the gulf we can't see. Before the passage on death being swallowed up in victory that I quoted above, Paul wrote, "The first Adam became a living being; the last Adam became a life-giving Spirit" (1 Corinthians 15:45). The first Adam of course was the Adam in Genesis, the man who represented the human race. He broke God's command and got us into the mess we're in now. Because of his sin, his descendants all lose the battle to corruption and death.

The last Adam, Jesus Christ, became a human being who was like us in every way. He endured all manner of human sufferings and died as a ransom on our behalf. God the Father punished his Son in our place and credited his righteousness to all who come to him in faith.

Because of Christ's work on the cross, my father, my wife, and my mother knew their final defeat would be their first step in God's final victory. As I founder in the grief riptide that has swept me out to shoreless waters, I cling to that truth like an exhausted swimmer holding on to a buoy. It's the hope that gives substance to faith. God will write the final chapter in the book. He's going to give those who know him a happy ending.

The written saying that Paul quoted, "Death is swallowed up in victory," is more than someone's opinion, like bad things occurring in threes. It's from the Scripture in the book of Isaiah. There the prophet wrote:

He will swallow up death in victory,
And the Lord God will wipe away tears from their faces.
He shall take away his people's rebuke from all the earth.
For the Lord has spoken.

—Isaiah 25:8

The Isaiah passage occurs within a hymn of praise to the Lord. In the broader context, Isaiah 24-27 is sometimes called the Isaianic Apocalypse because of its thematic similarity to Revelation: universal judgment, Israel's ultimate deliverance, and a call to trust in the LORD. Chapter 25 begins with the hymn of praise. At the opening of the chapter, Isaiah writes:

O LORD, you are my God.
I will exalt you; I will praise your name
You have done wonderful things;
Your counsels of old are faithfulness and truth.

—Isaiah 25:1

And what are God's wonderful things? Don't expect fluffy kittens. Instead, look for something that looks more like the white hats clearing the black hats from town. Here's the next verse.

For you have made a city a heap;
A defended city a ruin.
A palace of strangers no longer will be a city;
It will never be rebuilt.

—Isaiah 25:2

God is to be praised, even when he destroys. We don't know which city Isaiah had in mind. Apparently its particular identity wasn't as important as the destruction itself. From the cities came the ruthless and avaricious—those who trampled the innocent for personal gain. What mattered to Isaiah was the thoroughness of God's deliverance.

The results that emerge from the deliverance are impressive. When God establishes himself as the divine superpower, the strong nations will glorify him, and the cities will fear him. He will be the strength of the needy, giving them refuge from the storm and heat. He will kick out the squatters. He will prepare a lavish banquet for his people and remove the veil of half-truths and lies with which the oppressors had dominated them for so long (Isaiah 25:3-7). And finally, he will bring the threefold blessing mentioned in verse 8: swallowing up death in victory, wiping away tears from all the faces, and taking away his people's rebuke.

So why go into all this detail on an ancient Old Testament prophecy? Because Paul draws his readers to the Isaianic context when he quotes the passage. Personally, I'm glad he does. When it comes to death, I don't have time for any of the death-as-friend propaganda. It's no friend, and its presence is no time for celebration. Paul calls it what it is: the last enemy (1 Corinthians 15:26). Death has never taken prisoners, and it never will. It leaves weeping in its wake. It claimed my father, my wife, and my mother in the space of a year and a half, and I'm ready to watch it go down. Its own demise is the only worthy end.

Paul explained that Jesus Christ will bring the prophecy to pass when he returns to take his people home at the end of the age. In the same section of the letter, he gives us the foundation for our hope. Christ sealed the promise when he rose from the dead. He ate and drank with his disciples and invited them to put their fingers into the nail holes in his hands. His resurrection was real. After forty days, he ascended to heaven while they watched. Now he rules as sovereign Lord, superintending history until the appointed time to fulfill the promise takes place.

Then he will return to take his people home, where corruption and death will never touch them again. I'll see Mom, Dad, and Marie in the flesh, with my own eyes. The Lord himself has spoken.

Now that's a saying I can live with.

Journal

What wrong thinking and superstition have I been forced to swallow? Do I have a right to be angry at it and act against it? What truth can I muster to stand against its influence? How am I going to react to wrong thinking, whether it's my own or someone else's?

_____

_____

_____

_____

_____

_____

_____

_____

_____

_____

_____

_____

Sermon:

Philippians 3:4b-11
Losing Everything

Presentation to the Fellowship of Christian Athletes
Ashland University, September 18, 2007

Sermon: Philippians 3:4b-11
Losing Everything

Presentation to the Fellowship of Christian Athletes
Ashland University, September 18, 2007

Thank you for coming this evening. It's an honor to be able to speak to you. Before I begin with the text I've chosen, I'd like to ask you some questions to get an idea of where you're coming from.

- How many of you have had to make choices in your lives? I don't mean choices like, "Do I break up with Brenda because Susan is really hot and I think she likes me?" I mean serious choices.
- How many have had to make excruciatingly difficult choices?
- How many have had to make choices you knew would stay with you the rest of your life?

These questions take us into the subject for this evening. A *Sports Illustrated* article a few years ago featured interviews with world-class athletes who used performance-enhancing drugs. To a person, they said something like, "I'm approaching my peak athletic period, and I'm after a world record. If the drug kills me before I'm thirty, I don't care. The only thing that matters is the record."

Do you hear what they're saying? They've defined their whole being on the basis of that one thing. Their identity revolves around what probably will be a single chance, and most likely the window will come and go in a matter of minutes or seconds. If they get the record, their name will go into the sports journals. But they're jumping for the brass ring from thirty thousand feet without a parachute. If they miss the ring, it's not a matter of pass/fail. It's pass or nothing.

Let me ask you a couple of questions: How would you characterize your life? What defines you as a person?

- Athletic achievement?
- Popularity?
- Affirmation?
- Intellectual ability?
- Money?
- Security?
- Love?
- Fame?
- Recognition?
- Power?

I'm talking about a sense of being—the rock bottom denominator that says, "Distill all the other stuff out, and this my hope, my dream, my basic identity. This is what defines who I am." What is your personal everything? Now consider the alternatives. What would you do if you lost it? More importantly, can you imagine something valuable enough to compel you to give it up in exchange?

Part I—Paul, Who Lost All Things
A.   Paul at the Center of His World

This is the issue Paul brings up in his letter to the church at Philippi in Philippians 3. The book as a whole is a warm personal letter to the church. This issue drops into the middle of an otherwise upbeat narrative. Here is how he begins the section: "Finally, my brothers and sisters, rejoice in the Lord. To write the same things to you truly is not bothersome, and for you it is beneficial" (Phil. 3:1). So far, so good. Then Paul whacks them with three warnings, written to exploit their shock value. "Beware of the dogs, beware of evil workers, and beware of the circumcision" (Phil. 3:2).

We don't know the whole context, so we're left to fill in the blanks. Some of the internal clues indicate that the Philippians' faith had started to become more difficult than they had anticipated, and the believers had begun to get cold feet. We do know that the Roman culture was polytheistic, and Philippi was a thoroughly Roman city. In Rome everyone gave lip service to the emperor and to the local gods. The religious rules were simple and involved a certain measure of tolerance. First, Caesar is Lord. Hail Caesar. Second, honor the local deities. Third, worship whomever you want. No one cared what gods you believed in, as long as you didn't write off the local and national deities.

The apostle Paul, however, came preaching an entirely different message. The book of Acts records the history of the early church. Chapter 16 tells how he and his partner, Silas, came to the city and began to proclaim the ultimate write-off. Jesus Christ alone was Lord. Paul's message and works were compelling enough to split the popular opinion. Ultimately he and Silas were arrested, thrown into prison, and beaten. Instead of giving in, however, they persuaded the chief jailer and his family to become believers. Many began to say, "I think these guys are right" and put their faith in Christ as Supreme God of the universe.

This is where we begin to speculate, but the scenario fits what we know. The new Christians worshiped Christ alone and took the idols down from the shrines in their homes and shops. They no longer declared, "Hail Caesar." When their friends and customers came in and saw the empty mantels, they began to distance themselves. These Christians denied the gods, and worse, they denied Caesar. In the Roman mind, they had become atheists. The Christian disciples' once-thriving businesses began to decline, and they found they no longer could feed their families. They didn't realize their faith was going to be this difficult.

Then someone apparently thought of the perfect solution. What if they had themselves circumcised and became proselyte Jews? Everybody knew that Jews refused to bow to Caesar, and Rome gave them a wide berth. Therefore, if the Philippian believers changed their ethnic persuasion, they could function relatively normally as citizens. To the rest of the world, they would be Jews. Meanwhile they would continue to treasure their true identities as Christians.[9]

Paul didn't buy the idea. He had fought for the purity of the gospel at great cost, and part of that purity involved Christ's free grace being offered to Jew and Gentile alike, regardless of anyone's ethnic background. In other words, if Gentiles had to become proselyte Jews to be Christians, the gospel of free grace could not be true. This is the context for the denunciation, "Beware of the dogs, beware of evil workers, and beware of those who practice circumcision." The remark refers to any Jews who claimed that salvation required ethnic re-identification. In direct contrast to them, he declared three contrasting points, "For we are the true circumcision, who worship God by the Spirit and glory in Christ Jesus, and who place no confidence in the flesh." (Phil. 3: 3). This set up his case against the Philippians' hope to get away with proselyte circumcision.

In verses 4 through 11, Paul presents his autobiography—the main part of his case. It consists of three parts. The first section covers what his life looked like when he was bound up in Judaism, and it was a formidable act. Paul was a world-record performer in his day. Next he told how he lost everything from his old life. Finally he told the church why he was happy with the trade.

The section is structured differently than what we're used to reading. A common method in ancient times was to set up the argument symmetrically, so that the sections come together in an A-B-A' fashion. This was called chiastic form. Imagine a stepladder with rungs on both sides. The top of the ladder becomes the main point. Everything else is built around it. Paul's argument walks up one side of the ladder, presents the high point in the middle, and finishes it by climbing back down the other side.

The thrust of the argument is this: where the Philippian believers thought they could hold to Jewish and Christian ideals at the same time, Paul saw them capitulating. They were about to trade their hope in Christ for confidence in the flesh.

To demonstrate his case, he argued in terms of degree. The Philippian believers hoped to become a little Jewish and leverage their Christianity against it. But Paul had been altogether Jewish and had given it all up for Christ. If they wanted to build a case, they needed to outdo Paul on Jewishness. Of course, that would be like a little league baseball team going against an American League pitcher, and Paul didn't hesitate to throw an American League three-pitch strikeout. This is the essentially the purpose of the segue, "Though I also could have confidence in the flesh. If anyone else thinks he can put confidence in the flesh, I can do more" (Phil. 3:4).

The words, "I can do more," introduce his case. The A section begins with a recitation of the seven most cherished marks of his Jewish life—four arising from his pedigree and three showcasing his accomplishments. You want Jewish? Paul was heroically so. Verses 6 and 7 summarize Paul's pedigree as a free Jewish male.

- He was circumcised the eighth day according to the strict observance of the Law of Moses.
- He was an Israelite by birth. And if you don't think nationality is important, hum a few bars from Bruce Springsteen's "Born in the USA," or ask a union worker what he or she thinks about NAFTA, the North American Free Trade Agreement. Nationalism always will be alive and well.
- He came from the tribe of Benjamin, which held bragging rights for some notable accomplishments. Chief among them was King Saul of the Old Testament, who became Israel's first king. Paul's Hebrew name was Saul, after his nation's first king.
- He was a Hebrew of Hebrews. There's no stray blood in this guy's veins. He was a registered purebred.

You may be thinking that Paul was showing off his silver spoon in his mouth. He was. If the saying, "Whoever dies with the most toys wins," is true, so is its corollary: whoever is born with the most toys has a nice head start. Paul was born at the front of the pack. He didn't rest on his credentials, however. He took advantage of his native privilege and built some serious dividends on it. The next three points show his accomplishments.

- You want law keeping? Paul was a Pharisee. These guys were the most self-disciplined men of their day. They were the religious athletes—guys who could quote the Bible and law codes for hours on end. Their "everything" consisted of their intellectual and moral accomplishments. In the Jewish world, no one knew the technical nuances of religion the way the Pharisees did.
- In terms of zeal, Saul was fanatical. When this new religion that called itself "the way" arose, he was determined to wipe it from the face of the earth. This guy carried Christians' blood on his hands, and he was proud of it. According to the book of Acts, the old Saul was a raging bull. When Acts introduces him, it says he was "breathing out threats of slaughter against the Lord's disciples" (Acts 9:1).
- Finally he had self-righteousness based on law keeping down pat. If there were such a thing as world-class self-righteousness, Paul had it.

> Watch the judges' scorecards come up. Ten-point-oh, ten-point-oh, ten-point-oh, ten-point-oh . . .

Paul's religion was his identity. He was well bred, religious, zealous, and self-sufficient. His world record medal lay in his religious accomplishments. He was the center of his universe, and he challenged the Philippian believers to do better.

The first pitch was a fastball in the dead center of the strike zone. It smacked into the catcher's mitt before the batter even saw it coming. Strike one.

B. The Real Center

Why did Paul bring all this up for the Philippians? Because he wanted to show his readers how steep the grading curve was. If they wanted to rely on Jewishness, they had to step up to a level of play they didn't even know existed.

So what happened? In the short version, Paul lost his personal everything in an instant. When the old Saul was on the road to Damascus, carrying papers authorizing him to seize and bind anyone who belonged to the way, Christ appeared to him in a light so brilliant it left him blinded for four days. During the encounter, a voice said, "Saul, Saul, why are you persecuting me?"

The dumbfounded man could muster only, "Who are you, Lord?"

And the Lord said, "I am Jesus, whom you are persecuting" (Acts 9:4-5).

The truth toppled his world. He realized Jesus really had risen from the dead, the religion he had been trying to destroy was true, and he had been wrong all along. His pedigree and accomplishments vanished. But Christ didn't leave him holding an empty bag. He filled it with his salvation, giving him a whole new life to be lived for the Savior.

The B section (Philippians 3:7-8) is a summary of that change. Before I read, though, I need to ask if there are any business majors or minors with us this evening. I want you to pay close attention to this section and tell me what Paul is doing. These verses form a smaller chiasmus within the larger chiasmus. The pinnacle of the entire argument lies at point d.

a   But whatever things were *gain* to me,

b   I *counted as loss* for Christ.

c   In fact, I *count* all things as *loss* . . .

d   For the excellency of the *worth* of knowing Christ Jesus my Lord . . .

c'   For whom I have suffered the *loss* of all things.

b'   I *count* them as refuse,

a'   That I may *gain* Christ . . .

Gains, losses, counting—he was writing his ledger and balancing his books. On the one hand, he had lost his personal everything. The things he valued above everything else had evaporated. On the other, what he once thought was worthless has become his most valuable possession. And at the very top was the crown jewel—"the excellency of the worth of knowing Christ Jesus my Lord." Some versions use the word "value." It's the thing worth more than anything else—his gold medal, his reason for living.

His old "everything" was now gone, but he didn't care. When he held it up against the surpassing worth of knowing Christ, everything else had become rubbish. The term in the original language is stronger than that. It's the material we flush into the septic tank.

Another fastball down the middle, and the batter never moved. Strike two.

A'. Paul's Shared Life with Christ

For the third and final section of his argument, Paul took his readers down the other side of the stepladder. The A' section is a mirror image of the A section—seven points held face to face against his earlier accomplishments.

Here he threw a curveball. First, over against his three former lifetime accomplishments he held up three gains that he never could have received outside of Jesus (v. 9):

- He is found in Christ, not having *his own righteousness* that comes from the law . . .
- But that which is through *faith in Christ* . . .
- The *righteousness* that is from God and obtained by *faith*.

These points show why I call his last ball a curveball. On the surface it sounds like sour grapes. His old life was ripped off, so he settled for what was left.

This wasn't the case for Paul, however. His old law-keeping righteousness might have been impressive, but all his life he had walked a moral razor's edge. He would have lost everything with a single moral slip.

Let me give you an example. When I was in college, O. J. Simpson was one of the most respected names in the sports business. His career as a football player had been stellar. To add to that, he was photogenic and comfortable in front of the camera. He knew his sport and could communicate it well. He made the transition from player to expert commentator seamlessly. Major corporations fell all over themselves to get him to advertise for them. Of course you know what happened. He fell from grace and became a laughingstock.

This is what Paul is saying. No matter how great his past works were, they couldn't hold him up. He was always one slip away from losing it all. On the other hand, his righteousness under Christ was something he could never earn, but it also was something he could never lose. Now he didn't have to work day after day, hour after hour, and minute after minute to keep his balloon inflated. He could rest in Christ. Paul's righteousness lay outside of himself. It rested on simple faith that came from God. He couldn't do better than that.

Second, at the conclusion of his autobiography, he built four contrasting points to mirror his pedigree. They focus on his brotherhood with Christ. Verses 10 and 11 read, "That I may know him, and the power of his resurrection, and the fellowship of his sufferings, being made conformable unto his death, so that by any means I might attain unto the resurrection of the dead."

- He wanted to know *Christ,*
- To know the power of *his resurrection,*
- To participate in *his sufferings,*
- And to become like him in *his death.*

Wait a minute, Paul. You traded your accolades for suffering and death? Are you nuts?

Paul would say, "No, I traded my accolades for his suffering, death, and resurrection. Christ suffered infinitely for me so he could impart life to me through his resurrection. How can I give him less than my life in return?"

The first line summarizes everything: "that I may know him." For many of us, our college period is the time when we discover the guy or girl we want to spend our lives with. We prepare to make a commitment that will redefine us for the rest of our lives. The person we choose becomes the most important person in the world to us, and we want to do everything we can to know him or her. Paul is that serious about Christ.

- When we come to know Christ, the first way we know him is through his resurrection. This only makes sense, because it's the risen Christ who introduces himself to us.
- But he is not just the resurrected Christ. He suffered and died first. Therefore, if we want to know him intimately, we're going to have to know suffering and dying as well, because the power of the resurrection is bound up with suffering and dying.
- Do you realize that everything Christ accomplished while he lived on the earth, he accomplished by suffering? He learned how to empathize with humanity because he suffered as a human being. He knows how to rescue us when we struggle with temptation because he endured the same things we have to endure. Finally, he paid the price for the sins of his people by suffering on the cross.

If we belong to Christ, we will be called to suffer. It's part of the message of the gospel. He suffered to know us intimately and to secure our salvation. We must suffer to know Christ intimately. As we experience pain, loss, betrayal, grief, and a whole host of other emotions that strip us of everything we were certain was essential to our characters, Christ becomes the bedrock reality over everything else. Suffering takes our sense of self-sufficiency and exposes it for the counterfeit bill that it is. Suffering drives us to Christ.

But when we know Christ, our suffering becomes a meaningful experience. One of the things suffering accomplishes is to help us connect with others who go through difficulties. At the beginning of the school year, when finals and term papers are a semester away, you don't think about things like this. When it's three in the morning and your world had just fallen apart, we gain a new perspective. Do you go looking for the party guy or girl who always gets the laughs? Or do you think, *Hey, Lindsey has had to deal with this problem. I wonder if she'll mind if I wake her up to talk.* When you do, you'll discover a deeper friend in Lindsey than you ever thought possible. Then someday you'll be able to do the same for someone else. Suffering builds character in us that attracts people when they need help the most.

Okay, so what? Where is Paul going with all this?

He wanted to show the Philippian believers two things. The first is his autobiographical statement in verse 11—". . . if by any means I might be able to attain the resurrection of the dead." His sense of indebtedness to Christ was infinite. Christ had given his blood for Paul's salvation. Paul could give back nothing less than his life.

The second point comes in verse 17. This verse forms the moral of the story. We're skipping a few verses, but the line of reasoning is easy to follow. You can read it at your leisure. Paul wrote, "Join together in following my example, brothers and sisters, and just as you have us as a model, keep your eyes on those who live as we do." Paul the Major League player had to humiliate the Philippians with the strikeout pitches. Afterward he wanted to come alongside them and lead them to a deeper sense of maturity. If we expand Paul's words, he would be saying, "Don't be half-followers of Christ. Be my true brothers and sisters, and follow my present example. Name Christ openly, and take the heat."

Part II—The Moral of the Story: Those Who Have Lost All Things
So what does this mean for you as twenty-first-century college students? Are you supposed to abandon your college plans and hopes so you can become hermits?

Absolutely not. Christ never calls anyone to a dumbed-down religion. I can tell you this, however: When Christ confronts you with the words, "Follow me," he doesn't come to negotiate. He's not a salesman with a slick pitch. He comes as King to announce his sovereign rule over you. His call for you to enter into discipleship is absolute. He commands your entire allegiance.

That doesn't mean he comes in and takes over like a tyrant. He will compensate you. He will initiate you into a brother- and sisterhood that will become closer than family. He will give you a sense of purpose more satisfying than anything in the world of academia, notoriety, wealth, or sports could offer in twenty lifetimes. And he will grant you the rest of eternity to enjoy fellowship with him.

These appear to be intangibles at first, but let's apply Paul's math to our present situations. I include myself here. In a hundred years, the now-current academic papers won't appear even in anyone's footnotes. In a hundred years, the world will have devoured at least the twentieth generation younger, more energetic, and better-looking celebrity, with no more memory of our contemporary household names than yesterday's morning dew. Our wealth will belong to someone who won't care how hard we worked to generate it. And someone else will have captured the athletic records. All our earth-bound prizes will be gone. Only Christ remains after everything else evaporates.

You can mark this as well: when we make a decision to follow Christ, we have to leave our future in his hands. I can't tell you that you will lose everything, any more than I can guarantee you won't. I know you will suffer difficulty because everyone does. It's part of life. Following Christ will come at a cost. I can tell you this, however: On the basis of Scripture[10] and personal experience, whatever Christ takes from you, he will compensate with blessings infinitely more valuable. I'll close with some examples of those who gained greater opportunities to give to others as a result of their suffering.

The Church at Philippi

We've left the church at Philippi hanging, so we'll address the members there first. Paul filled whatever wiggle room the Christians there thought they might have had with concrete. His concluding admonition to them was, "Follow my example" (Philippians 3:17). With a presentation like the one they had received, they had little choice but to follow.

We don't have a return letter from the Philippian church, so we can't know for certain how they received his letter. The Bible does give us a hint about their response, however. In 2 Corinthians 8, part of a later letter to another church in Greece, Paul found it necessary to remind the Corinthian believers about a relief offering they had pledged to collect for the Jerusalem church. A severe famine had hit the Jerusalem area, and the church there was desperate. The Corinthian church had taken up a pledge drive but began to lag in its sense of urgency to provide their promised gift. As an incentive—and frankly, as a way to shame them—Paul told them about the

Macedonian churches, which included the one at Philippi. He wrote, "With an overwhelming burden of hardship in their deep poverty, and yet with great joy, they proved their generosity" (2 Corinthians 8:2). The text goes on to say that the Macedonian churches begged him to allow them to give beyond even their meager means.

The phrase "overwhelming burden of hardship that came from their deep poverty" is the telling one. In their pre-Christian lives, the Philippians were the business leaders in their community. The purple fabrics that came from one of the early converts at Philippi (Acts 16:14) were prized by statesmen. They were the Saks Fifth Avenue merchandise of their day. Now, apparently these once-wealthy church members struggled to survive.

Did they suffer the loss of all things?

Absolutely. But in exchange they found the priceless privilege of being aware of what was going on among Christians around the world, along with the joy of contributing to one of the earliest Christian relief movements in church history.

The Apostle Paul

We discussed Paul's loss of all things. He talks about his loss plainly. If we look closely at his list, however, there's not an immediately tangible thing among his losses. Yet the things he lost make mere belongings pale in comparison. He gave up:

- His academic and religious reputation
- A massive sense of self-worth
- A self-image that defined him every waking moment
- A pedigree and self-discipline that he had built to world-class levels
- His cause for boasting

This kind of résumé was a blank check. His qualifications would cause the people in the high-ranking religious echelons to drool. In the end, however, he called it bodily waste in comparison to what he found. In their place he gained:

- Christ's name
- Unconditional acceptance in Christ

- A spiritual foundation laid in stone
- A sense of meaning that came from outside himself
- A cause to live in humility

The turning point in Paul's life revolved around his loss of all things, but his compensation was infinite. In his younger days, Paul was driven by his lust for earned perfection. Those who didn't share his worldview drove him into a rage. He was passionate but with a passion driven by anger. After his conversion, his driving force came from the joy that Christ had rescued him from himself.

My Story

Some of you know my story. In November 2002, I woke up to find my wife Marie doubled over in pain in the bathroom. I took her to the emergency room, where doctors began tests. By that afternoon, we learned that she had stage-four colon cancer. She died five months later.

About a year after that, while my daughter and grandson were still living with me, my grandson began to show symptoms of severe lethargy. Ultimately tests determined that my house had lead-based paint inside and out, and Ben was suffering with lead poisoning. He was teething and had ingested the paint when he chewed on the window sills. The levels in his system were in danger of causing permanent brain and kidney damage. Thankfully we discovered the problem before his health failure became irreversible, and he was able to make a full recovery.

I didn't fare so well. The State of Ohio Department of Health issued an order for me to have lead abatement done on my house. They gave me no compensation. I had to take out a $35,000 loan under duress, knowing I did not have the means to pay for it. After the abatement was completed, I sold the house, although this has not begun to pay the debt. Patty, now my wife, has taken on the debt with me, but we will be in its shadow for years.

Have I suffered the loss of all things?

I have made Philippians 3:8 my life verse. But my gain has been immeasurable. The experience has opened repeated doors to offer compassion toward others who suffer loss. That may not sound like much, but it is something I cherish. I could not have acquired the gift any other way than through the emotional gauntlet I had to endure.

My Daughter's Best Friend

When my middle daughter's best friend was in her early twenties, her husband was killed in a car accident. The other driver was drunk and high. At the trial, she learned that he was driving on a suspended license and lapsed insurance. Yet after a twenty-minute deliberation, the jury declared, "Not guilty." Now she raises her son alone.

Has she suffered the loss of all things?

She would give anything to have her husband restored to her. Nor is her journey finished. Though the incident occurred about five years ago, she still struggles with deep acceptance issues. I bring up her story to emphasize two points. First, I am not trying to advocate a fast track to spiritual wellness. God never calls us to put on a spiritual happy face a month after a tragedy. Suffering can be brutal, and we are no less spiritual when we have to admit that we suffer. Second, my daughter's friend illustrates a deeper truth in the Christian life, and that is the genuineness of her faith. In spite of her theological struggles, she has not abandoned her faith. I do not doubt that the Lord will complete the work he has started in her and that she will become a great comforter to others someday. I pray for her eventual restoration.

Lou, a Man I Met Last Week

Last week I met a middle-aged man at the seminary. His name was Lou. Lou had crashed and burned after drug use, and his first wife left him. After getting his life back together, he remarried and planned to live a relatively quiet life with his second wife. Last year, however, they learned that his wife's CPA had embezzled her life savings. A month later, authorities found the CPA face down in a river in Europe. Lou and his wife have no hope of recovering their money, and Lou has about two months of his pension left.

Has he suffered the loss of all things?

He's lost his whole life, yet when I talked with him, his sense of joy showed a depth of courage I have seen in very few people. He has a dream to plant a church. People don't make the leap from that kind of depth to the awareness of Christ's compensation without that compensation being real.

Conclusion

These are some who have learned to live as Paul did. I give them to you so you can see the variety in Christ's grace. For anyone who suffers great loss, that person's "everything" will be unique. Watch the person closely. With a unique loss, he or she will have an equally unique gain in Christ. A giant will emerge from the rubble.

Part 3

Hope Triumphant

Friday, March 3

Two Years after Passing

Faith, Hope, and Grief

And these, having obtained witness through faith, did not receive the promise—God having provided something better for us, so that they would not be made perfect without us.

—Hebrews 11:39-40

For eighteen years, Marie and I co-owned a locksmith business, the enterprise that my father started. After she died, I passed the business down to my son-in-law. One of the last service calls I performed before he took it over occurred in late autumn, for a 92-year-old lady. I don't remember what I did on the call, but our conversation will remain with me the rest of my life.

She had a worn Bible on her coffee table. I mentioned it and asked if she was a Christian. She was. We began to share our faith then, and I discovered that she had uncommon depth. She also was a widow, which gave us both our circumstances and our faith as points of common ground. I'd been thinking about Hebrews 11, so I shared my thoughts about Marie and her relationship with the heroes of faith—what they all might perceive from heaven and how they interpreted it.

My customer's answer surprised me. She said, "Oh, I don't think so. She's with Christ, and his glory is the greatest thing we could imagine. I doubt that anyone there is even aware of what's going on here."

Her answer caught me off guard. Yes, Christ's glory will be the greatest thing we'll see in eternity, far eclipsing all other glories. And since I lacked a chapter-and-verse proof text with which I could counter, "But see, here it says," I had to defer to her opinion. For the next several months, I imagined my wife sitting before God's throne, enraptured in Christ without another thought or care. I tried to believe that neither she nor any of the other witnesses in Hebrews 11 would be concerned with the history unfolding beneath them. We who live on the earth have God alone as our audience.

A disconcerting phenomenon began to occur. While my customer's argument was logically convincing, it left me with a growing emotional hole. If Marie had lost all memory of our present reality, then our connection to each other was severed. My sense of hope began to shrivel. For a while I slogged on, telling myself, *Put the loss behind you and try not to think about it for now.* That tactic failed, and I began to search the Bible to see if it had anything to say about the subject.

It did. Now I'm ready to reclaim my ground. No one particular passage changed my mind, but the material in Hebrews 11-12, along with the book of Revelation, played an important part in helping me reassert my original position. Here's my case. Hebrews 12:1 reads, "Therefore, since we are enclosed by such a great cloud of witnesses, let us lay aside every weight and the sin that so easily besets us, and let us run with endurance the race that is set before us."

Our understanding of this passage will revolve around the way we define the term *witnesses*. If they appear only as a list of names placed in chapter 11 for our perusal and edification, they stand as little more than museum pieces. On the other hand, if they are active characters who play a role in our present-day walk in faith, they have the potential to bring about a much more profound impact on our lives.

Taken alone, the Greek word for *witness* suggests a those-who-once-were-there role. The word is *martureo* (mar-tur-EH-o), from which we obtain our modern word *martyr*. Many saints did die for their faith, as Hebrews 11:35-37 acknowledges, but the word doesn't restrict itself to those who have lost their lives. Various Bibles have translated the term in this verse "good report" (King James), "approval" (New American Standard), or "commended" (New International). In other words, witnesses are not necessarily martyrs, or even eyewitnesses. All who authenticate their beliefs through their actions join the ranks as witnesses to the faith.

I surmise that my elder sister in the Lord understood Hebrews 12:1 this way. The phrase in Hebrews 11:39, "having obtained witness through the faith," lends itself to this interpretation. In this context, the words sound a note of finality. Our predecessors fought the good fight, and God was pleased with them. Those saints have finished their course and are able to rest in God's glory. Their work is complete, and only their testimony ties them to our own faith walk. If this were all the Scripture we had, I would have to affirm my elder sister's interpretation.

If this were all we had.

Two points from the junction of Hebrews 11 and 12 argue for an interpretation that understands an active role for the Old Testament witnesses. The first one we'll look at is the meaning of the word *enclosed* in Hebrews 12:1.

The author of Hebrews was a master of his language, and he chose his words deliberately. Hebrews 12:1, referring to the members in the faith honor roll in chapter 11, says we are enclosed by them. The word is a particularly strong one. Mark 9:42 and Luke 17:2 use it in connection with the horrifying end for the person who causes Jesus' little ones to stumble in their faith. There Jesus says it would be better for him to have a millstone *tied* around his neck and be drowned in the sea. In Acts 28:20, the apostle Paul, a prisoner under Roman guard, uses the word to describe how he is *bound* by his chain. And the author of Hebrews uses the word earlier in his letter in Hebrews 5:2. A high priest, he argues, is able to be faithful precisely because he shares the same basic nature as the people he serves. Specifically, because he is *beset* with infirmity, he is able to exercise compassion toward others who struggle in their walk.

Let's return to Hebrews 12:1 with these meanings. We are tied, bound, and even beset by the witnesses in chapter 11. In other words, they're here to stay. To use a modern figure of speech, they corral us. Whatever we do, right or wrong, we do in their shadow.

This word offers strong evidence for an active role by the witnesses, but by itself it's not yet compelling. The second point, a phrase in chapter 11, is. The sentence spanning Hebrews 11:39-40 reads, "And these, having obtained witness through faith (from the word, *martureo*), did not receive the promise—God having provided something better for us, so that they would not be made perfect without us."

We can see the marks of an educated man in this writing. The author has put a lot of content into a short space—four strands, to be exact. To make it easier to understand, let's pull them out and examine each separately. The author refers to two groups of people and marks them by the pronouns, "these" and "us." The former refer to the Old Testament saints. The latter are the New Testament saints—both during the days of the letter and by implication, the saints now living. The statement draws the two groups into association with each other. Here are the four arguments in the list. The points of comparison are in italics.

- "These" [the Old Testament saints] *did* obtain witness through their faith.
- But they did *not* receive the promise.
- Through their incompleteness, God has provided something *better* for *us*.
- Specifically, the better thing for us is that *their* perfection remains incomplete without us.

The first two statements deal strictly with the Old Testament saints, and they're straightforward. They *did* obtain witness through their faith, but they did *not* receive the promise.

Let's consider the implications of this. If the Old Testament saints' testimony as witnesses were a stand-alone edifice, as my elder sister believes, then their work would be complete. They would have received everything for which they labored, including the promise. But as Hebrews says, the promise has eluded them.

This draws us to the second pair of facts. The reason why the Old Testament saints wait for the promise is because God has provided something better for us through their imperfection.

This is interesting. Since they are yet incomplete, we would expect the text to say, "God having provided something better for *them*." Instead, he made the provision for us. The writer states his case negatively for effect: "So that they would not be made perfect without us." The meaning becomes clearer when we state it positively. They wait for us to complete our race so they can receive their promise.

Let's look at Hebrews 12:1 again in this context, where the author urges us to continue the race in light of our spiritual predecessors' anticipation. "Therefore, seeing that we are enclosed by so great a cloud of witnesses, let us lay aside every hindrance, and the sin that so easily overwhelms us, and let us run the race that is set before us with patience."

The witnesses most definitely do see us. They enclose us because they wait for us to finish the race they started. Their reward depends on how well we run. With their own ultimate completion tied to our finish, is it any wonder they should corral us? They can't win until we cross the finish line. This is why the author calls us in chapter 12 to run our part of the race diligently. It's not just our own.

Let me give you an example. I was a track runner in high school, but I just did not have any natural speed. Because of my impediment, I stuck to the distance runs where speed wasn't such a critical factor. In my senior year, my school hosted an invitational meet, with around fifteen teams competing. For reasons that baffle me to this day, my coach assigned me to be the anchor runner for the four-mile relay. A relay race consists of four runners, each running his or her respective distance in turn. The runner carries a baton, a stick about an inch and a quarter in diameter and a little over eleven inches long, and passes it on to the next runner as he or she completes the respective leg of the race. The anchor runner is the last to run.

Because time is such a critical factor, the team members pass the baton on the run. The baton pass is an art. The runners have a specified distance on the track in which to pass it. The one receiving the baton times his or her start to correspond with the previous runner's finish. If anyone drops the baton at any time or even carries it beyond the allotted passing space, the entire team is disqualified. Finally, the race goes to the team with the lowest total time. This makes the anchor runner the most critical person on the event. Because a four-mile relay is so long, the anchor runner's strategy becomes even more important.

I was mediocre as a two-miler and hopeless for any lesser distance. To pace myself at a strong mile pace required a full-out sprint. I knew the outcome before the race began.

The first three runners were brilliant. One, a walk-on that year, posted the fastest time on the team. When my leg of the race came up, we were in first place. I gave the race my best effort, but my best effort was a two-mile pace that wasn't even close to what a mile pace needed to be. By the time we finished, I had put us in last place. The team lost because of my failure.

The author of Hebrews is telling his audience, "You're the anchor runners in this history-long relay, and the rest of the team depends on you. Don't squander their race."

To offer a more positive metaphor, I believe God is arranging his saints' faith into a kind of historical quilt. Like the quilt maker's materials, no single piece possesses any glory in itself, but when all the pieces come together under a master quilt maker's hands, the effect is breathtaking. Further, the quilt isn't done until the last piece is sewn into place. The first pieces can't manifest their full splendor outside of the whole. Might God then be building us, saint by saint, into a grand work of art, knitting us together across geography and time, waiting to present us to the world as a witness to his goodness at the end of the age?

Two Scriptures support this claim. The first is from 1 Thessalonians. The saints in the Thessalonian church, who believed Jesus would return during their lifetimes, found themselves blindsided when their family members began to die. To bolster their hope, Paul wrote, "God will bring those who sleep in Jesus with him . . . and the dead in Christ shall rise first. Then we who are alive and remain shall be caught up together with them in the clouds to meet the Lord in the air. So shall we ever be with the Lord" (1 Thessalonians 4:14b, 16b-17).

The dead and the living are to be reunited. For this promise to carry any meaningful weight, the living must believe they will be able to recognize the ones with whom they will be reunited. Granted, their relationship with their loved ones will change (Matthew 22:30), but their earthly identities will remain. Eternity, therefore, bears the imprint of history.

The second Scripture is from Revelation 6:9-11, which describes the fifth seal judgment. The first four seals reveal the famous horsemen of the Apocalypse. But when the Lamb breaks the fifth seal on the scroll, we jump from earth to heaven, where we see the martyrs under the throne, crying, "How long, O Lord, holy and true, will you wait to judge and avenge our blood on those who dwell on the earth?" (Revelation 6:10). Have you ever wondered about that? Why does God devote a seal—a whole seventh share of the title deed to the universe—to a prayer meeting at the foot of the altar?

Actually, this event marks an important turning point in the course of Revelation, and it's marked by the care with which John treats it. God gives the martyrs white robes and tells them to rest a while longer, until the number of their fellow servants "who would be killed as they were, should be fulfilled" (Revelation 6:11). From this point, the book revolves around the conflict between heaven and earth. The beast rages in its blood lust for the saints while God casts down ever more gruesome judgments on those who hate him. Meanwhile, heaven watches the terrestrial drama in wonder.

Two passages show us the cosmic drama written large. The first is in Revelation 8:1-5, when the Lamb opens the seventh seal of the scroll. John writes that heaven was silent for about half an hour. The commentators are in agreement that this is stunned silence over what is about to occur on the earth. The images of the coming judgment are vivid. Seven angels holding trumpets come before the throne, waiting to sound the next set of judgments. But they don't begin without ceremony. An eighth angel emerges with a golden censor and takes his position before the altar. Here he offers incense with the prayers of the saints before the throne. Doubtless many of these prayers are the pleadings from the slain martyrs of Revelation 6:9-10. Then the angel does a curious thing. He takes the censor, fills it with fire from the altar, and throws it to the earth.

This is not a picture of rejection. It's a picture of affirmation. God calls his saints' prayers as a witness against their enemies, and his affirmation is so appalling that it causes atmospheric and geologic upheaval. The cosmos itself cannot contain his judgment. From this point on, Revelation shifts back and forth between God's judgment and the unsaved world's anger.

The climactic moment occurs in Revelation 19, when the martyrs' number reaches completion and God brings down Babylon, the world system that is so gluttonous for the saints' blood. Now the redeemed sing, "True and righteous are his judgments, for he has judged the great harlot who corrupted the earth with her fornication, *and has avenged the blood of his servants at her hand*" (Revelation 19:2, emphasis added). Between Revelation 6 and 19—for thirteen chapters—heaven watches while God brings history to a close. When the final curtain drops, the effect is cosmic. Here the final hallelujah chorus is a doxology offered to God because he has answered the martyrs' prayer from Revelation 6.

We can draw three implications from this. First, the unresolved conflicts on earth resonate all the way to heaven. In fact, the book of Revelation hinges on this prayer that is waiting for resolution. It sounds in heaven as a plea for justice on the earth, and when the final answer does come, heaven rejoices. Second, heaven cannot be satisfied until justice is restored on the earth. This is the point of the book. No one rests in heaven until God closes history in justice. Finally, as we move from Revelation 19 to the last two chapters of the book, we see the New Jerusalem come down from heaven. It can do so only after the administration of justice on the earth opens the way for it. In other words, time and eternity reunite only after the cosmic conflict achieves resolution.

This shouldn't be surprising when we consider how the God of eternity has written his legacy in time. He created in history. "In six days the LORD made the heaven, the earth, the sea, and everything in them" (Exodus 20:11). He redeemed in history. "When the fullness of time came, God sent forth his Son" (Galatians 4:4). He also promises to judge in history. "He has appointed a day in which he will judge the world in righteousness" (Acts 17:31). Yes, the Lord is to be honored for who he is, but he is equally praiseworthy for what he does. History matters to eternity.

The Revelation account shows the saints' history written large at the end of the age. Revelation's later martyrs will bring closure to their predecessors in the same way we are called to complete the faith of those who have gone before us. If this is true, then its corollary follows. Revelation's early martyrs hold their breath while they watch their brothers and sisters contend to the death for their collective faith. Why, then, shouldn't those who have gone before us watch with equal excitement to see how we complete their race?

This understanding replants the backbone in my hope. I have reason to pick up my pace again because I know Marie and all the other saints watch from heaven. The collective body corrals us. The Scripture invites us to listen for their cheers.

Journal

As I think about issues that bridge history and eternity, what part does the Bible play in shaping my thinking? How do I know I will be with God at the end of my earthly life?

_____

_____

_____

_____

_____

_____

_____

_____

_____

_____

_____

_____

Afterword

Thank you for reading this book. Chances are, if you have read this far, you have experienced grief or tragedy in your own life. My hope has been to help people like you who have suffered these kinds of hardships.

If this book has helped you—or even if it hasn't—I'd love to know. Feel free to e-mail me at dougknox51@gmail.com. God bless you in your spiritual journey.

Bibliography

Becker, Amy Julia. "Boundaries in Grief: Why Medicine Should Never Trade Places With a Time to Properly Mourn," *Christianity Today* Online, August 22, 2010. http://www.christianitytoday.com/ct/2010/augustweb-only/43-51.0.html (accessed August 22, 2010).

Kübler-Ross, Elisabeth. Grief Cycle Model. http://www.businessballs.com/elisabeth_kubler_ross_five_stages_of_grief.htm (accessed November 18, 2011).

Mowinckel, Sigmund. *The Psalms in Israel's Worship*, The Biblical Resource Series. Grand Rapids, MI: Eerdmans, 2004.

Oakes, Peter, "Re-mapping the Universe: Paul and the Emperor in I Thessalonians and Philippians." *Journal for the Study of the New Testament* 27, no 3 (March): 301-22.

Terrien, Samuel. *The Psalms: Strophic Structure and Theological Commentary*, Grand Rapids, MI: Eerdmans Publishing Company, 2003.

Endnotes

1. Amy Julia Becker, "Boundaries in Grief: Why Medicine Should Never Trade Places With a Time to Properly Mourn," *Christianity Today* Online, August 22, 2010. Downloaded from http://www.christianitytoday.com/ct/2010/augustweb-only/43-51.0.html (accessed August 22, 2010).

2. Sigmund Mowinckel, *The Psalms in Israel's Worship*, The Biblical Resource Series, ed. Astrid B. Beck (Grand Rapids, MI: Eerdmans, 2004), 28.

3. Samuel Terrien, *The Psalms: Strophic Structure and Theological Commentary* (Grand Rapids: Eerdmans Publishing Company, 2003), 356.

4. Elisabeth Kübler-Ross, "Kübler-Ross—Five Stages of Grief," http://www.businessballs.com/elisabeth_kubler_ross_five_stages_of_grief.htm (accessed November 18, 2011).

5. Sigmund Mowinckel, *The Psalms in Israel's Worship*, 196-97.

6. Samuel Terrien, *The Psalms*, 356.

7. Ibid., 361.

8. The mass destruction took place during the wilderness wanderings and is recorded in Numbers 11-25.

9. For a full treatment of this hypothesis, see Peter Oakes, "Re-mapping the Universe: Paul and the Emperor in I Thessalonians and Philippians." *Journal for the Study of the New Testament* 27, no 3 (March): 301-22.

10. Second Corinthians 1:3-10 is the classic passage that discusses the way our mutual suffering allows us to bring comfort to others who suffer.